subUrbia

ERIC BOGOSIAN

THEATRE COMMUNICATIONS GROUP

1995

Bogosian, Eric.
SubUrbia / Eric Bogosian.—1st ed.
ISBN 1-55936-101-8
1. Young adults—United States—Drama.   2. Suburban life—United
States—Drama.   3. Generation X—Drama.   I. Title.
PS3552.O46S83   1995
812'.54—dc20   94-44840
CIP

Book design and composition by The Sarabande Press

First Edition, April 1995
Fifth Printing, September 2001

To André Bishop, a man of faith

INTRODUCTION

I grew up in Woburn, Mass., about ten miles northwest of Boston. Like most suburbs, its history is a nasty collision between past, present and future.

A stately Methodist church, a small green with a "Minuteman" and a stone library grace the center of the city. So does a small marker memorializing the men who died in the Vietnam war. The local myth is that two hundred years earlier Paul Revere rode through what is now a strip of woods separating the housing developments.

In the late 1800s my hometown was a hotbed of Industrial Revolution-type activity. (Rubber was first vulcanized in Woburn!) Because of the lax environmental laws in the bad old days, the soil in parts of Woburn is among the most toxic in the whole United States.

Our fair town has seen mayors indicted for corruption, has given birth to top football and hockey teams. Nancy Kerrigan is from one town over.

Woburn has grown from being an aging industrial hamlet to a teeming professional community intersected by I-95's high-tech corridor. America's first really big shopping mall was built out off the highway. When I was sixteen, I hung out at that mall and shopped for Hush Puppies. When I was twenty and a college dropout I worked at the new Gap store. Now I go there and get nostalgic.

As I was growing up, as the mall and the high-tech factories were built, the local roads and highways got busier and busier. Thirty years ago the mini-mall where I first hung out, "Four Corners," had a barber shop, a pharmacy and a furniture store. Now a 7-Eleven, a Burger King and a car dealership stand in their place. Looking at Four Corners now, it's hard to believe anyone ever had a personal feeling for the place. But I did. It's where I came of age. I fell in love there, got drunk there, got in fights. (One time, Mikey Turner bit a chunk out of me in the parking lot of the Dunkin' Donuts. Had the scar for six years.)

For the people who first moved to Woburn, the suburbs represented escape, fresh air, order and lack of crime. But for those of us who grew up in the suburbs, the suburbs didn't *represent* anything, they *were* something: home. Suburbs were not an escape from reality, they were reality.

Not until I went to school in Chicago, did I realize there was any place *not* like Woburn. My home is a strange home, a home full of contradictions. A community, but not a community, a place, but not a place. And as Joel Garreau points out in his study *Edge City*: a city, but not a city. (One of the chapters is devoted to our local mall and environs.)

This territory is where I come from, where lots of other people come from, too. If you grow up in the suburbs, you are told over and over again that you are living the American Dream. But if you are like me, you're not so sure. If you are like me, you leave the American Dream.

The strangest aspect of growing up where I grew up is thinking you know everything about the world, when in fact you know nothing. This is the story of me and mine, as it continues today, all over America.

ACKNOWLEDGEMENTS

subUrbia started out when my friend, Bob Riley, then at the Institute of Contemporary Art in Boston, suggested I try something larger than solo work. Fred Zollo had been encouraging me for years to write about the town we grew up in, and so with a grant from the Massachusetts Council on the Arts and Humanities, the play began sometime around 1986. Later Bob Brustein was kind enough to let me "workshop" the initial writing on the piece with his students at the American Repertory Theatre in Cambridge. That was in 1989. And again, in 1992, Anne Cattaneo arranged a workshop production with students at Juilliard.

Many people have helped shape this play, nudged it toward the magnificent production it received at Lincoln Center Theater in 1994. I would like to thank:

At the Institute of Contemporary Art in Boston: Bob Riley and David Ross.

At A.R.T: Bob Brustein, Rob Orchard, Julie Miles, Rebecca Rickman; the cast—Ellen Kohrman, Ross Salinger, Chris Colt,

Steve Zahn, Celeste Ciulla, Sean Runnette, Dean Harrison; and my assistant, Jeff Zinn.

At Juilliard: Michael Kahn, my invaluable stage manager Pat Sosnow, Clifford Berek, Isaac Ho, George Xenos, Chele Ware, Caroline Seltzer, Lisa Renee, and the cast—Maya Thomas, Chris McKinney, C.J. Wilson, Brian Kelly, Jeff Stafford, Carrie Preston, Loren Lovett, Dallas Roberts, Nicole Marcks, Danny Mastrogiorgio.

Recipe for a brilliant, mind-altering production: start with script, add Robert Falls, fold in a totally driven, young-genius cast. Set blender speed at "whiplash" and wait for the subscribers to walk out. Thank you Bob, Firdous, Tim, Josh, Wendy, Zak, Martha, Reneé, Samia and Steve—you made my dream come true.

Heartfelt thanks to Bernie and André and to our wonderful design team, Derek, Ken, Gabriel and John. To Annie Cattaneo for tea and sympathy. And to our ever-patient and loving production stage manager Christopher Wigle and stage manager Miriam Auerbach. Thanks to Liz Timperman for making sure this text was performance letter-perfect. And thanks to our sturdy understudies: Nick Rodgers, Jon Patrick Walker, Aasif Mandviwala, Maya Israel and Anney Giobbe.

Lincoln Center Theater is a big place. I'm sure I don't know everyone who made this show go. Until I do, special thanks to Daniel Swee, Jean Bacharach, Steve Callahan, Ed Nelson, Julie Crosby, Patrick Herold, Mari Eckroate, Mala Yee, Jeff Hamlin, Merle Debuskey, Susan Chicoine, David Leong, Julia Judge, Beth Emelson, Alison Laslett, Norma Fire, Graeme McDonnell, Bonnie Runk.

One final point on the Lincoln Center production of this text: Zak Orth wrote and played the music that accompanied my lyrics on the songs. And Samia Shoaib created the Urdu text as spoken by her character. Martha Plimpton created her performance from my text. And Tim Guinee and Steve Zahn did all their own stunts.

Of course, none of this could have succeeded without an amazing director. Robert Falls had the vision and strength to pull this circus together. I can't thank him enough.

Special thanks to all my good friends who make it work: George Lane, Michael Carlisle, Ron Taft, Philip Rinaldi, and Edith Meeks.

Thanks to Terry Nemeth at TCG and to my obsessive and care-giving editor, Steve Samuels.

Finally thanks to Jo Bonney, my muse, conscience and love.

If you would like to learn more about "subUrbia" or other work by Eric Bogosian, please visit his homepage at www.ericbogosian.com.

subUrbia

subUrbia received its world premiere as part of the Festival of New American Plays at Lincoln Center Theater, under the direction of André Bishop and Bernard Gersten, May 22, 1994. Sets by Derek McLane, costumes by Gabriel Berry, lighting by Kenneth Posner, sound by John Gromada, fight direction by David Leong and direction by Robert Falls. The cast, in order of appearance, was as follows:

TIM	*Tim Guinee*
BUFF	*Steve Zahn*
JEFF	*Josh Hamilton*
NORMAN CHAUDRY	*Firdous E. Bamji*
PAKEEZA	*Samia Shoaib*
BEE-BEE	*Wendy Hoopes*
SOOZE	*Martha Plimpton*
PONY	*Zak Orth*
ERICA	*Babette Reneé Props*

Contemporary recorded music is used throughout the play. Since music is always changing, the production should use music that is loud, energetic and helpful to the direction of the play. I also refer to costume elements, but these don't need to be taken literally. New clothing styles and music are always surfacing. Each character is more or less hip about his or her style of dress and it is up to the director, designer and actors to find the clothes that make sense.

ACT

ONE

*Out of black, loud music surges at the audience, getting
louder. Music cuts out as:*

    *Lights up on the sidewalk along the side of a 7-Eleven-
type convenience store. At an angle, some of the store inte-
rior is visible upstage right, but for the most part we are
facing a large whitewashed cinder-block wall. "Behind"
the store, stage left, against the "rear" wall, is a large
dumpster, sitting in shadows. Hung along the wall of the
store, at the corner where the front meets the wall, is a pay
phone, stage right. A small bench runs along the wall next
to the phone. The area stretching out toward the audience
and into the wings is asphalt pavement, demarcated with
yellow parking lines. A large cement curb sits along the
extreme downstage edge of the stage.*

    *Tim Mitchum, twenty-one years old, is sitting on the
sidewalk near the phone, his back to the wall, drinking a
beer, smoking a cigarette. His hair is short and his t-shirt
reveals an athletic body. Next to him is the rest of a six-
pack, two pair of rollerblades and a puck, a pair of sneakers and, propped against the wall, three hockey sticks.*

Norman Chaudry, twenty-four, and his sister Pakeesa, twenty, can be seen at work within the 7-Eleven. He's at the counter reading a book as he eats something from a bowl. She's in traditional Pakistani dress, cleaning the cooler cases with Fantastik.

Loud music blares as first Buff Macleod on rollerblades, and then Jeff Gallagher walking, enter from downstage right, each holding a slice of pizza in his hand. The music emanates from the boom box Buff is carrying.

Both are about twenty years old. Buff affects a loose "homie" style of dress, while Jeff is simply dressed in dark clothing of no particular style. His hair is messy, as if he just woke up.

Buff snaps off the boom box and deposits it on the sidewalk, continuing to roll around in circles as they talk.

BUFF *(To Tim)*: Hey you! Get a job!

JEFF: *This* is fucking hot.

BUFF: Drip the grease off, man! The grease is the main problem!

(Jeff contemplates his slice, still too hot to eat. Tim stoically ignores the clowning)

JEFF: If I had to live on pizza, beer and nothing else, I could do it.

BUFF: Vegetables, minerals, cheese and pepperoni. All four food groups, man.

JEFF: Like eating a megavitamin.

BUFF: Like eating Madonna.

(Buff takes a bite, chews with his mouth open. Jeff takes a big bite, burns his tongue as his slice falls on the ground)

JEFF: AAAHHHHH!   MOTHERFUCKER-COCKSUCKING-
SHIT-SHIT-SHIT! *(Stomps his slice with his boot)*
BUFF: Yo! It's the master of discipline!

(Jeff flips his slice offstage, jogs into the 7-Eleven and grabs a bag of Oreos and a six-pack. Buff talks to no one in particular. Tim drinks)

There was this show on the other day about Asia and shit. They had these Tibetan dudes, man. Like how they pray and do their thing. They just like sit on pillows for hours. And they do this weird singing:

(Buff proceeds to make this outlandish nasal droning, with surprising expertise, mimicking the Tibetan monks. Jeff has dropped some bills on the counter and comes back out of the store. Norman, holding his plastic bowl and a spoon, chewing a mouthful of food, speaking with a strong Pakistani accent, follows Jeff)

NORMAN: Hey! Seven-twenty!
JEFF: Huh?
NORMAN: Seven-twenty!
JEFF: I gave it to you!

(Buff interrupts his droning and stands up)

BUFF: He paid you, man!

NORMAN: You owe me twenty cents. Seven-twenty! Seven-twenty!

BUFF: Yo! You're spitting rice all over me!

(Jeff reaches into his pocket and hands twenty cents to Norman who, with a last look of disdain, returns to his store and his meal. Jeff sits down on the bench)

JEFF: Guy should cut down on his caffeine intake.

BUFF: Needs some pizza in his diet.

(Buff skates past Tim)

TIM: Fucker's got an attitude. Somebody oughta crack his dot-head with a baseball bat. And remove the skates, asshole, before I break both your legs.

BUFF: Fascist! You're a fascist, man! Neo-fascist.

TIM: Sit down, you're embarrassing me.

JEFF: I guess the guy's just nervous. Stranger in a strange land.

BUFF: I went in there yesterday, he was practicing the pledge of allegiance. Boning up for the big test.

TIM: That's depressing.

JEFF: He's from a Third World country. I respect him for that.

TIM: Spare me that "Third World" shit.

JEFF: That's what you call it.

TIM: I've been to the "Third World," man. It smells like you wiped your ass and made a country out of the paper. The people are dog-eating, monkey-faced greaseballs.

(Buff sits next to Tim and removes his skates, exchanging them for his sneakers)

JEFF: He's a human being. You gotta give him that.

TIM: Only thing I gotta give him is a one-way ticket back to greaseball-land.

JEFF: He wants to be like us.

TIM: Good luck. We'd get back to base after a weekend in Manila, they'd take our clothes, soak 'em in gasoline just to kill the bugs. Eat an ice cube over there, you got the shits for a week.

JEFF: Those places are screwed up 'cause we fuck them up.

TIM: Who's "we?"

JEFF: The American Empire. The Air Force. You. Me.

TIM: The gooks did it to themselves, pal. You have no idea, fucking chaos on a stick.

BUFF: But like, isn't he from Arabia or some shit like that? You're not a gook if you're from Arabia, man.

JEFF: He's from India. The whole family's from India. India and Saudi Arabia aren't even the same continents, jerky!

TIM: The C.O.'s used to give us that shit. "Don't confuse the Thai with the Filipino. It offends them. Don't confuse the Chinese with the Vietnamese." Bullshit. They're all the same. Subhuman.

(As he munches Oreos, Jeff watches Buff finish his pizza)

JEFF: Yeah, well, that pizza could feed a family of four back in India or Turkey or wherever the fuck he comes from.

BUFF: But, how would you ship it there, man? Federal Express? By the time it got there it would be way cold and coagulated. Total waste. Cheese would be all stuck to the cardboard.

JEFF: Buffster, that slice you're chomping on is the difference between life and death for some half-dead Bangladeshi.

BUFF: Yo man, you're getting me all upset here.

JEFF: You *should* get upset! Everyone should get upset. When Hitler was greasing the Jews, people were saying "Don't get me upset! You're bumming me out!" It's my duty as a human being to get pissed off. Not that it makes any difference in the first place. Nothing ever fucking changes. Fifty years from now, we'll all be dead and there'll be new people standing here drinking beer and eating pizza, bitching and moaning about the price of Oreos and they won't even know we were ever here. And fifty years after that, those suckers will be dust and bones. And then there will more suckers after them. And all these generations of suckers will try to figure out what the fuck they were doing on this fucking planet and they will all be full of shit. It's all so fucking futile!

(Tim is lying on his back by now)

TIM: If it's so fucking futile what the fuck are you so fucking upset about, fuckhead?

JEFF: I'm fucking alienated.

(Jeff stands and paces. Buff follows on his heels)

BUFF: Me, too! I'm alienated, too. But at least there's Oreos. *(Grabbing an Oreo)* Oreos, the perfect dessert after the perfect fucking meal! Dark and chocolatey on the outside, white and delicious on the inside. You can eat them whole, or you can split 'em in two, and scrape off the creamy frosting with your teeth.

(Jeff won't let it rest)

JEFF: SARAJEVO! HAITI! ARMENIA! You ever watch the
news, Buffman? There's a world outside this tarpit of stu-
pidity. Empty, void, stupid. It's the end of the world, man—
no ideas, no hope, no future. The fucking apocalypse.
You don't even know what "apocalypse" means, do you,
Buff-cake?

(Buff will not be patronized)

BUFF: Of course I do, man. It was a movie. I saw it. Vietnam.
Martin Sheen. Marlon Brando. Surfing. Snails crawling on
razor blades. "This is the end," dum-dum-dum, "My only
friend, the end . . ."

*(Incongruously, Tim raises his voice almost sermon-like.
Buff continues to sing the melody under)*

TIM: "And in those days shall men seek death and shall not find
it; and shall desire to die, death shall flee from them."
Saint John the Disciple wrote Apocalypse. Check your
Bible.

BUFF: My Mom bought this toilet paper with Bible sayings
printed on it, but I told her like if the Pope came by and
had to take a shit we'd all get excommunicated and sent
to hell.

*(Jeff has found a seat on the downstage curb, his back to
the audience. Tim, having grabbed another beer, is sitting
on the bench facing him. Buff sits next to Tim, happily
munching Oreos)*

JEFF: Yeah, yeah, it's all a big joke. It's because of the Pope that
       the world is crawling with starving people. Ever heard of
       the slums of Rio?

TIM: What about Calcutta?

JEFF *(Not getting the reference)*: Huh?

TIM: Pope doesn't have much pull in India.

JEFF: Well, that's an exception.

TIM: What about China? About a billion starving people there
      in China.

JEFF: So what's your point?

TIM: What's *your* point?

JEFF: Forget it. I'm just saying . . .

TIM: Yeah?

JEFF: Things are fucked up and no one cares.

TIM: Things are fine with me. How are things with you Buff?

BUFF *(Happily munching)*: Excellent.

(Jeff stands up, pacing, enamored of his own eloquence)

JEFF: Fuck the Pope! One half of the world is starving to death
       and the other half is hooked up to their VCR cathode ray
       tubes absorbing nonstop porno and violence, sucking
       down high cholesterol food-fat, getting larger and larger
       and larger like a bunch of Christmas geese ultimately
       bursting with cancer and bad karma.

TIM: Christmas geese? What the fuck?

JEFF: They force-feed geese to make goose liver pate. It forces
       their livers to enlarge. We're turning into geese. That's
       what I'm saying, obviously.

TIM: You learn this at Carver Community College? You took a
      course in decadence? "Decadence 101."

JEFF: No! I learned it on Sesame Street. They jammed a funnel down Big Bird and pounded the granola down his gizzard.

(Jeff deflates. Buff is bopping around)

BUFF: Every morning while I'm doing my abs I check out Sesame Street. There's this babe on the show, she's like a total fox. Does porno tapes on the side.

(Jeff sits next to Tim on the bench)

JEFF: An actress on Sesame Street does porno tapes.

BUFF: I saw it, man. With my own dick. There's this place you can go to in town, it's got like forty-eight channels of triple-X porn. Push buttons with one hand, choke the chicken with the other. Hey, speaking of choking the chicken, I saw "the Duck" in Topper's yesterday.

JEFF: "The Duck?"

BUFF: You know, the guy who could blow himself.

(Buff squeezes himself onto the bench with Jeff and Tim)

JEFF: What's he doing these days, he still blowing himself?

TIM: He's a teaching assistant at a Catholic Girl's High School. Physical Education.

(Jeff can't help but smile. Tim likewise has dropped his mask)

BUFF: No. Really? Does he really? That is so cool!

(Long pause)

JEFF: Remember Fred Pierce? Buff says he's gay now.

TIM: Fred Pierce? Fred Pierce was the best running back we had, no way was he a fag.

(Buff restlessly stands, checks himself out in the plate-glass reflection)

BUFF: Yeah, well he isn't running anymore. He's in Mercy Memorial. Moms told me he has AIDS. She was praying for him and shit. Even lit a candle down Saint Barbara's.

JEFF: Tim, didn't you kick his ass one time?

TIM: It was nothing. I lost a tooth, he took ten stitches. He's not gay. No one who can punch like that is a 'mo.

BUFF: I'm telling ya, man. Donnie was in town and Pierce tried to pick him up in a bar. Didn't know Donnie was from Burnfield. Tried to take him to a hotel room!

TIM *(Beat)*: And you're saying he has AIDS?

BUFF: Shit's going around, man. Don't wrap the meat, it don't stay fresh.

(Buff comes a little too close to Tim on the last line and Tim tags him with a quick punch as Buff dances away)

JEFF: I keep thinking about Mister Fresher. Best teacher I ever had. Turned me on to *Steppenwolf* and *Naked Lunch*. The only teacher I cared about in high school and he dies of alcohol poisoning. How does that happen?

BUFF: You drink a shitload of vodka, man.

TIM: Fresher was a loser. Lived in a dream world. Ever hear him talk about Woodstock? Whoa! Probably prayed he would go out choking on his own vomit so he could die like his heroes. He's choking on his own puke and he's thinking "Just like Jimi, man, just like Jimi!"

BUFF: "'Scuse me while I kiss the sky!" Dum-dum-dum-dee-dee-dee-duh-duh-duh. *(Mime air-guitar followed by mime puking)* BLAARRGGHHHHH!

TIM: Fresher was bound to fail. He was too delicate. It's a liability in this world. People like him become the statistics. The stupid, the delicate, the weak. Like Pierce.

JEFF: Why was Pierce stupid?

TIM: He couldn't keep his butt shut.

JEFF: That has nothing to do with whether you're stupid or not. Alot of geniuses were gay. Sometimes I wish I was gay. It would make my life simpler.

(Buff is on the ground doing push-ups)

BUFF: Stop staring at my butt, man!

JEFF: Hey, man, homosexuals get laid alot more than straight normal people. That's all they do is get laid. Must be nice, you want to poke someone, you just say, "Yo, want to get poked?" "Sure do!" "OK, let's go!"

TIM: My fantasy.

JEFF: You don't have to be with one person all the time, don't have to always be worrying about what they *think*, what they *want*. You're free. To do what you want.

TIM: Trouble with the little lady, Jeffrey?

JEFF: I didn't say that.

BUFF: Hey, Jeff, how's Sooze?

TIM: Yes, Jeff, how's Sooze?

JEFF: Who brought up Sooze?

TIM: You did.

JEFF: I did not.

TIM: Sooze is too good for you, Jeff. That's the problem. A man should never be with a woman whose vocabulary is larger than his.

JEFF: My . . . then must be why you're stuck by yourself.

TIM: My lifestyle is pure choice, pal. I'm striking a balance between Nietzsche and Bukowski.

BUFF: How's her friend?

JEFF: Bee-Bee?

BUFF: Yeah, "Bee-Bee." She's got a nice smile, that Bee-Bee.

JEFF: If you're so interested in her, ask her yourself.

(Buff jumps up)

BUFF: I'm at work yesterday, bitch comes in, orders a 12″ pie with extra cheese, so I asked her if she wanted me to like carry it out to her car . . . right? Bitch is obviously in heat. Says "yes" right away. So I carry the pie out to her car. We smoke a J, she blows me, we eat the pizza, I chase it with a beer. Smoke, babe, slice, brew—all four bases—fucking home run, man.

(Jeff gets up and goes to the pay phone and dials)

JEFF: Buff, your ability to fantasize is only exceeded by your ability to lie.

(Buff follows him, climbs up onto the pay phone)

BUFF: Untrue, Jeffster. Last week I picked up two nymphets at the Soundgarden concert. Two on one. I swear. You can ask them. I got their numbers.

(Jeff grabs an imaginary prick and jerks it up and down)

TIM: Fuckin' Pierce. I knew something was wrong with him. Must have been why we blew the playoffs.

(Jeff listens to the phone while talking to Tim)

JEFF *(Into the phone)*: It's me. What are we doing? I'm down the corner. With Tim and Buff. Nothing. What about, you know. . . . Well, I thought you were getting your mother's car? Oh. You gonna pick me up?

(Tim throws his beer bottle off towards the dumpster. Buff flips the boom box on, LOUD. He picks up the hockey stick and starts fucking with Tim. Tim grabs the stick. They start wrestling as Jeff continues to talk on the phone)

JEFF: So did you talk to him? Did you tell him we couldn't afford twenty bucks a ticket and why didn't he put us on the comp list? There's always a comp list. Bullshit.

(Norman comes out of the 7-Eleven)

NORMAN: Hey, you guys! You can't be out here all night tonight.

(They ignore him. Norman walks over and turns off the boom box)

BUFF: We're just having a
conversation.

NORMAN: This is private
property.

BUFF: Hey, this is America,
man, don't tell us
about private prop-
erty, OK?

NORMAN: You gotta go
now! The customers
complain.

BUFF: *We're* your custo-
mers, man. We're not
complaining.

NORMAN: Please!

JEFF *(On the phone)*: So
what did you tell him?
That's harder. So
what . . . we're just
supposed to hang
around until he shows
up? Why can't you. . . .
Why won't your moth-
er let you keep the
car? Alright. Alright.
I said alright. Drive
over here and I'll take
you back later or
something. We'll get
my Dad's Cherokee.

(Buff turns the boom box on again. He and Tim get into an almost absurd slam-dance. Norm watches helplessly, finally turning the music off once more. Jeff hangs up the phone and turns on Norman)

JEFF: I was talking to my mother who is in the hospital dying
of terminal cancer, that OK with you?

NORMAN: So go visit her if she's in hospital.

BUFF: You dissin' his mother, man?

(Pakeesa, from within the store, taps on the window and holds up a portable phone, indicating there's a call for Norman. With a look of disgust on his face, Norman turns from them and goes into the store. When he takes the phone from Pakeesa his demeanor changes and he becomes

*chatty on the phone, laughing, his eyes still on Tim, Buff
and Jeff)*

TIM: Who you talking to?
JEFF: Nobody. Sooze.
BUFF: Sooze coming down?

(Jeff bends over to tie his shoe)

JEFF: Maybe. Uh . . . it's my birthday. This week. She's coming
       by to wish me happy birthday.
BUFF: Your birthday? Well shit!

*(Jeff's still bent over as Buff grabs him by the rump and
starts "humping him" while singing off-key)*

HAPPY BIRTHDAY TO YOU!
HAPPY BIRTHDAY TO YOU!

*(This starts a mock fight, with Jeff grabbing Buff in a head-
lock and the two of them hopping around, trying to get the
upper hand. Buff keeps singing throughout. Tim joins in,
humping Buff. The three hurtle around the stage locked in
a bizarre mock-fuck-fight)*

BUFF AND TIM:
       HAPPY BIRTHDAY DEAR JEFFY!
       HAPPY BIRTHDAY TO YOU!

*(Bee-Bee enters. She's wearing a tie-dyed shirt, black
jeans, shag haircut, high-laced Doc Martens, a tattoo on*

one arm. The cluster-fight barrels into Bee-Bee and breaks apart)

BEE-BEE: Hey! Watch it asshole!
JEFF: He's the asshole!

(Uninterested, Bee-Bee sits on the bench and lights a cigarette)

BEE-BEE: What did Sooze say, is Pony coming?
JEFF: I don't know.

(Buff gives Bee-Bee a big smile and sidles up to her)

BUFF: Wanna beer?
BEE-BEE: No thanks. I don't drink. What did she say? Did she talk
    to Pony?
TIM: "Pony?" "Pony?" What's a "pony?" You mean the geek who
    played folk music at the senior prom? What's his name, Neil
    Moynihan?
BUFF: Pony's band Dream Girl's been on the road opening for
    Midnight Whore. Stadiums, man! So, Pony's coming by here?
BEE-BEE *(To Tim)*: Didn't you see their video on MTV?
TIM: I shot my TV.
BUFF: So, Pony's coming by?
JEFF: And anyway, now he's back and I thought maybe we'd get
    together tonight. And, you know, talk. That's all. No big deal.
    Me, him and Sooze. . .
TIM: Uh-huh. You wanted to get together with your close friend,
    Pony, the rock star? Sure, I understand. You want us to leave?
JEFF: No. We're gonna go someplace or something.

BEE-BEE: We are?

JEFF: She told him to come here. Fuck.

BUFF: Pony's coming?

JEFF: Don't ask me, ask Sooze.

TIM: If you want to be alone with Pony, Jeff, it's alright with us.

JEFF: It was just something we were going to do.

TIM: No, I mean, you two should be alone together. Talk about old times. Have some laughs. Warm your hands by the fire. Bond. Network.

BUFF: When?

JEFF: It's not like that. I don't give a shit.

TIM: Sure you do.

JEFF: I don't even like his music that much. But we were friends.

TIM: When were you friends?

JEFF: Sooze wants to see him.

TIM: Oh, *I* want to see him, too!

BUFF: We *all* want to see him. When is he coming?

BEE-BEE: Yeah, when's he coming?

JEFF: Later.

> *(Blackout: loud metal over.*
>
> *In the darkness, the silhouettes of the actors can be seen moving into new positions. It's almost a dance.*
>
> *Lights up on Sooze standing in front of the wall, sipping from a take-out container of coffee. She's offset her pretty face and shapely body by wearing shapeless black clothing and boots.*
>
> *Jeff, Tim, Buff and Bee-Bee are sitting on crates, the curb, etc., watching Sooze perform with flat aggressive intensity.*

*[Performance note: The actress performing this "piece"
has to make it her own. Odd props and costume pieces can
work])*

SOOZE: ONE: I look into the mirror, what do I see? Tits. Eyes.
Teeth. Cunt. Smile baby smile. Jiggle those tits. Spread
those lips. Give the boys what they want.

TWO: I stick a knife in my hand, what do I see? Blood.
Red and sticky as anybody else's. Any man. Any African-
Americans. Any slaves. I bang my head, what do I hear?
Silence.

THREE: Fuck Oliver Stone. Fuck Bill Clinton. Fuck
Howard Stern. Fuck Michael Bolton. Fuck Bryant Gum-
ball. Fuck Pope John Paul. Fuck my Dad. Fuck the men.
Fuck the men. Fuck all the men.

FOUR: What is a Man's Good Time? A piece of ass. A
hard ball. A porno tape. A hamburger with ketchup and
sperm spread all over it.

BUFF: Yummy!

SOOZE *(Losing her place)*: Oh shit.

BEE-BEE *(Coaching)*: "What are you looking at?"

SOOZE: Oh yeah. FIVE: Hey what are you looking at asshole?
You want some of this? You like this? Here you go.
(Spreads her legs, shows her butt) Here's the hole. Jump
on in. Or do you just want to look?

SIX: Bang your head, blow your nose, run down the
street, suck a hose / Chew my lips, eat some shit, eat a stick
of dynamite and blow yourself to bits / Shut your mouth,
go away, drink my piss, have a nice day / I hope you cry
and never doubt I hope you die with blood in your mouth,
I hope your lies will no more shout what's in my eyes

what's in your snout / you are a pig I know that's true / I
dance a jig fuck you fuck you fuck you fuck you fuck you!

(Pause. Sooze sips from her coffee)

JEFF: Is that supposed to be about me?

SOOZE: Slides go with it. Behind me.

BEE-BEE: It's called "Burger Manifesto: Part I—The Dialecti-
cal Exposition of Testosterone," isn't that a great title?

JEFF: Is that supposed to be about me?

BEE-BEE: We're thinking of using "Ween." Is that too much?

SOOZE: Why is everything about you, Jeff?

JEFF: Not everything. This. I *am* the man in your life.

SOOZE: "Man?"

JEFF: Yeah, "man," male, significant other, whatever the fuck
I am.

TIM: Phallic symbol.

JEFF: Phallic symbol. *(Thinks)* No.

SOOZE: It's a piece!

JEFF *(Walking away)*: A piece.

SOOZE: So, do you think it's good?

TIM: It needs some work, but it has promise. When do we get
to see the completed opus?

SOOZE: I'm not actually doing it anywhere, I'm just compos-
ing it as part of my application to the School of Visual
Arts . . . in New York.

BUFF *(Cracking a beer)*: Sooze, you know people in New York?

SOOZE: No. I'll just go. *(Pause)* I figure the worst I could do is
starve to death.

(Sooze glances at Jeff)

JEFF: "The worst I could do is starve to death." Listen to you!

SOOZE: I don't want to hear it.

JEFF: Because you haven't a fucking clue! You're all ready to pack your bags and leap into the unknown because some conceptual artist who teaches at a community college is having a midlife crisis and wants to sleep with a girl half his age so he tells you you have "talent."

SOOZE: Mr. Brooks is not a conceptual artist. He's a site-specific performance studies instructor. He's had shows in New York. He knows. He got reviewed in *Artforum*.

JEFF: He got reviewed in *Artforum*. Well, then you better listen to him.

SOOZE: Fuck, might as well not do anything. No one should do anything. Let's just stick our thumbs up our ass and twirl!

TIM *(Applauding)*: Bravo. Go to New York and make art Sooze. They need you. They need your unique point of view.

SOOZE: At least I have a point of view. I stand for something. I am trying to communicate something.

TIM: That's right. You are.

JEFF: What are you trying to communicate? Tell us.

SOOZE: So you can give me more shit?

JEFF: I'm asking an honest question. What are you trying to communicate?

SOOZE: I am trying to communicate how I feel. You know. Raise consciousness. Make people think for a change.

JEFF: You're going to make people think?

SOOZE *(Frustrated)*: YES, YOU ASSHOLE!

JEFF: About *what*?

SOOZE: About things that are important to me. Sexual politics, racism, the military-industrial complex. Things!

JEFF: Racism? You don't know anybody who's black!

SOOZE: Of course I do!

JEFF: Name one.

SOOZE: Karen Johnson.

JEFF: One.

SOOZE: You completely miss the point. I'm talking about idealism!

BEE-BEE: Responsibility! Progress!

JEFF: Idealism is guilty, middle-class bullshit.

SOOZE: *Cynicism* is bullshit.

JEFF: I'm not being cynical. I'm being honest.

SOOZE: But do you stand for anything? What? What do you stand for?

TIM: Go get 'em Sooze.

JEFF: I stand for honesty. Some level of . . .

SOOZE: Yeah, right.

JEFF: Let me talk!

BEE-BEE: What a dildo!

SOOZE: Fuck you.

(Sooze and Bee-Bee sit near each other, ignoring Jeff)

JEFF: Let me talk!

SOOZE: All you know is what's good for you. Typical male.

JEFF: Can I talk?

SOOZE: Tim, he listens to you. Do you think it's a good idea. Seriously.

TIM: It's a good idea.

SOOZE: Thank you. See, he did it. He left. He got his ass out of here.

(Tim takes a swig. Pause)

TIM: I did. I expanded my horizons. I served my country, and
      I saw the world. I sowed my wild oats. And now I'm back.
      I've gained wisdom and now I'm back. Go, you have my
      blessing, child. Say "hi" to Jack Kerouac if you see him out
      there.

SOOZE: I can't wait till Pony gets here. Have a conversation
      with a human being.

JEFF: Since when did you get this big affection for the guy? You
      didn't even know him in school.

SOOZE: Of course I did! He sat right behind me in study hall.
      All we did is talk. He called *me*, remember?

JEFF: You used to make fun of him.

SOOZE: I did not. Now you're lying.

JEFF: If you love him so much, why didn't you go see him play?

SOOZE: Because you didn't want to pay for the tickets.

JEFF: There's a limit, Sooze. I'm not going to pay twenty bucks
      to see Neil Moynihan play in a band I helped start.

SOOZE: He's always been a nice guy and I like him.

JEFF, TIM AND BUFF: He's a geek.

(Buff is fiddling with one of the hockey sticks)

BUFF: I'm a *video* artist, man. I been making these tapes. I
      ripped off a camcorder up at the mall and I've been mak-
      ing these tapes. I thought, it could be, you know, some-
      thing I *do*. I sent one in to America's Funniest Home
      Videos.

TIM: Buff, the postmodern idiot savant! He will outdo us all!

*(Sooze turns on the boom box, loud. Norman comes out of
the store, a broom in his hand)*

NORMAN: That's it, that's it. I'm calling the police!

JEFF: We're just standing here!

NORMAN: You are trespassing.

BUFF: Call the cops, man. Call 'em right now! Maybe my cousin Jerry will show up. He'll definitely take your word against mine. You tell him about the trespassing, and I'll tell him about how you sell cigarettes to minors. We'll see who spends the night in jail.

NORMAN: I'm not joking, now. Let's go.

SOOZE: We're just standing here!

(Pakeesa watches from inside, concern on her face. She disappears into the back of the store)

NORMAN: Go stand someplace else.

BUFF: *You* stand someplace else, man! You stand someplace else. This is our corner. You don't fucking own it.

NORMAN: Yes, I do. I do own it. It's mine. And you don't belong here.

BUFF: *You* don't belong here, man. We were here before you.

(Tim is placidly sitting on top of the pay phone. He speaks without looking at Norman)

TIM: Why don't you go back where you come from, towel-head?

SOOZE: Tim!

TIM: What? You standing up for this gook? I'm sorry, "wog." I can smell him from here.

NORMAN: And what are you, you drunk! You just hang around . . . on my property!

(Tim jumps down and walks up to Norman, gets in his face)

TIM: Fuck you, fuckin' dot-head. Greasecake! Nigger! *(Daring him)* You want us to go? Make a move.

(Norman turns away to return to the store. Tim quickly cuts him off)

SOOZE: Jeff!

(Jeff does nothing)

Tim, you win, you have the largest penis, can we go now?

(Norman puts his hand on Tim's shoulder to get past him. Tim grabs it and whirls Norman around, throwing him across the stage)

TIM: Oh, come on, honey!

(Tim pushes Norman hard. Norman stumbles backward. Jeff jumps in to separate them)

JEFF: Hey! Hey! Hey!

(Buff pulls Jeff back)

BUFF: Let 'em fight. The dude wants it.
SOOZE: No! Hey, wait a minute! This is getting ridiculous.

(Tim and Norman square off, Norman holding the broom-stick as a lion-tamer might)

NORMAN: OK, OK. You drunken shit.

(Tim smiles, ready to do damage)

BEE-BEE: Tim, let's go. You're gonna hurt the guy!
NORMAN: You are the nigger!

(Tim glances back at Jeff, sees the hockey stick in Buff's hands, grabs it)

SOOZE: Tim, what are you doing!? Stop it! Jeff!!!

(Jeff does nothing)

TIM: You want to be an American? You should learn a sport!

(Tim feints two or three hockey moves to an imaginary puck. Norman has two hands on his broom now, holding it for protection)

This is called "hockey."

(Suddenly Tim steps forward, moving the puck, smashes into the broom as if "checking" Norman hard. Norman falls backwards onto the pavement. He starts to get up, Tim knocks him back down. Norman tries to fend him off with the broom, Tim grabs it to tug it away from him)

Hey, don't start crying now!

(Norman crawls backwards to get away from Tim as Tim hits the ground hard around him, chasing him. Suddenly: Pakeesa has emerged from the store and is pointing a .38 special at Tim's head)

PAKEESA *(In Urdu)*: Haramzadeh, madarachot. Seewer ka baacha! [Translation: "Filthy bastard, motherfucker. Son of a pig!"]

SOOZE: Oh, shit!

TIM: What's this? Your mother?

NORMAN: It's OK, Pakeesa. *(Pause)* Pakeesa, it's OK. Go back in the store. Go back.

BUFF: Yo, Mama, that thing loaded?

BEE-BEE: Let's go!

(Norman stands and brushes himself off)

BUFF: Tim, you think she's got bullets in that thing?

NORMAN: Come on, Pakeesa. It's OK. They're just joking around.

(Pakeesa's eyes shoot to Norman. She appraises Norman's condition)

BUFF: We were just screwing around. Like Mohammed said. Can't take a joke, man. *(To Pakeesa)* I hope you got a permit for that, Mama.

SOOZE: We're sorry, we'll go.

TIM: Pull the trigger bitch.

(Pakeesa is going toward the store, followed by Norman. Tim follows, taunting her)

TIM: Somebody pulls a gun, they should know what to do with it.

SOOZE: Come on, Bee-Bee, let's get away from these racist macho-fixated assholes.

(Bee-Bee starts to move off with Sooze. Buff grabs the hockey sticks)

TIM: Kill or be killed, comprende? You're gonna regret this, you brown bitch. Better kill me now while you have the chance.

(Buff moves past Tim)

BUFF: Fuck her. Let's go. Find some weed.

(Sooze and Bee-Bee are off. Norman succeeds in steering Pakeesa back into the store. He stands in the doorway. Tim turns to go with Buff, then walks up to Norman)

TIM *(Quietly, with menace)*: I can find you anytime.

(Buff and Tim leave. Jeff picks up some trash, drops it in a receptacle)

JEFF: Hey, man, I'm sorry . . . OK? He's drunk.

(Norman ignores Jeff. He's still watching in the direction of Tim and Buff)

BUFF *(Offstage)*: FUCKING DOT-HEAD!

JEFF: It's a misunderstanding. He's upset about something and he took it out on you.

(Norman turns to face him)

I'm not . . . I don't want to hurt you.

(Norman watches him)

I'm on your side, man. Really.

(Norman turns away and goes into the store. Music up loud. Jeff walks off)

ACT
TWO

The lights over the wall are on, but the 7-Eleven is closed and dark.

Bee-Bee is standing near the dumpster, eyes closed, nodding her head and dancing to the music of the boom box blasting a hard rocking song.

Buff comes in, sits on the bench and watches her. Bee-Bee stops when she sees him. Buff looks down at his feet, closes his eyes and nods his head to the music.

Bee-Bee resumes her "dance." Both are moving to the beat, apart, yet together.

The music stops. Bee-Bee approaches Buff and sits next to him.

BUFF: Hey.

BEE-BEE: Hey. Gimme a cigarette.

(Buff gives her a cigarette. They smoke in silence)

You made a video?

BUFF: What?

BEE-BEE: Nothin'. *(Walks away)*

BUFF: What?

BEE-BEE: You said you made a video. What's it about?

BUFF: It's not about anything.

BEE-BEE: Oh. What's on it?

BUFF: Stuff I got off the TV. The Jetsons. And some shit blowing up I saw on the news. Plus one day my Mom was praying and shit and she didn't see me watching and I videotaped her.

BEE-BEE: Yeah? Your mom praying?

(Pause)

BUFF: And a cloud.

BEE-BEE: A cloud?

BUFF: There was this cloud and I videotaped it.

BEE-BEE: Oh.

BUFF: I was doing 'shrooms and I saw this cloud. It looks excellent on the tape. It's like the video is my head. And everything, you know, is like in there that I see. My Moms and TV and the sky and plus I'm going to come down here one night and walk around inside the 7-Eleven with the camera. Tape shit.

BEE-BEE: That would be amazing.

(Bee-Bee's self-consciousness is evaporating. The two of them look into the darkened store and try to imagine the tape)

BUFF: Yeah. Like imagine the inside of the 7-Eleven but with music. I'll put music on—Sonic Youth . . .

BEE-BEE: Yes!

BUFF: Fugazi, Nine Inch Nails, Tony Bennett. . . . Plus one night when nobody noticed I turned the tape recorder on on my box, taped everybody talking, you know? So I'm putting some of that shit in, too.

BEE-BEE: What did I say?

BUFF: Uh. Nothin'. You know?

BEE-BEE: I wish I could see it.

BUFF *(Direct)*: You can see it. Whenever you want.

BEE-BEE: Yeah . . .

BUFF: Sure.

(Awkward pause. Bee-Bee walks away, confused by Buff's attention)

Don't you work at a hospital or something?

BEE-BEE: Yeah. I'm a nurse's aide at Mercy.

BUFF: You're a nurse?

BEE-BEE: No. I, you know, clean 'em up. Empty the bedpans. Sometimes I bring lunch. That kind of thing.

BUFF: Old people? Like with Alzheimer's? Really fucked up?

BEE-BEE: Some of 'em. Strokes. Alot of types I don't know what's wrong with 'em. They're not moving too much and they get kind of yellow. Usually they die if they're real yellow.

(Bee-Bee is randomly stepping up and down on the down-stage curb. Buff follows)

BUFF: Sounds like a total bummer.

BEE-BEE: No, it's not. I like it. I mean they're not all com-

pletely, you know, in a *coma*. They know when I'm help-
ing 'em. Fred Pierce? He's there. He's going blind. I guess
it's AIDS. We just had a birthday party for him last week.
Twenty-two years old. Doctor Patel says he'll die pretty
soon. But Fred's great to talk to. Fucking funny guy. Says
things like "Watch it or I'll bleed on you."

(By now they're both seated on the curb)

BUFF: Fred's going to die?

BEE-BEE: Well, you know, he's really sick.

BUFF: Yeah, but doesn't that, like, bother you?

BEE-BEE: Sure, but it's alot worse for him. I know he needs me,
you know, just to say "hi" and talk. I need him.

BUFF: I guess.

*(Buff lies back onto the curb. Pause. Bee-Bee follows. They
are both lying on the curb, looking up at the sky)*

What are you doing now?

BEE-BEE: Right now?

BUFF: Yeah.

BEE-BEE: Waiting, I guess. Maybe Pony will have a stretch
limo. You know?

BUFF: Yeah. *(Pause)* Wanna go out back, in the woods?

(Bee-Bee sits up)

BEE-BEE: Now?

(Buff sits up, looks at her)

BUFF: We could smoke a doob. Hang out.

(Bee-Bee considers this)

BEE-BEE: I don't do drugs.

(Buff lies back)

But I'll go back. OK?

(Buff sits up)

BUFF: Whatever you want.

(Tentatively, they both stand. Bee-Bee takes the boom box. Buff takes her hand and they exit upstage left behind the store.

Tim enters stage right, carrying a six-pack. He crosses the stage, puts the six-pack on the dumpster, climbs on top of the dumpster, grabs the six-pack, tosses it up onto the roof of the 7-Eleven, then hauls himself up onto the roof. Once on the roof, he pops a beer, watches the world at his feet, drains his beer and throws the can off the roof, where it hits the ground below. He lights a cigarette and lies back. Only the smoke from his cigarette is visible.

Another empty flies off the roof.

Jeff and Sooze enter in the middle of an animated conversation)

SOOZE: It was a racial incident!
JEFF: It was just something that got out of hand!

(Sooze looks incredulous)

It isn't like Tim was going to hurt the guy.

SOOZE: No?!

JEFF: *They* pulled a gun. They overreacted. Did anyone get hurt?

SOOZE: It got that close.

JEFF: But nothing happened. Believe me, if I thought anything really bad was going to happen, I would have done something.

SOOZE *(Curious)*: Yeah? What would you have done?

JEFF: I would have stopped it.

SOOZE: How?

JEFF: I would have done something. This is kind of hypothetical isn't it?

(Jeff puts his back against the phone and draws Sooze to him)

Can we drop this for two minutes? I haven't seen you all day.

(They kiss. Sooze turns and Jeff holds her close, kissing her neck. She's enjoying the embrace, but he's getting much more into it)

No one's here. Let's go around back to the van.

SOOZE: Not the van! It smells in there. . . . Yech! Moldy old blankets, beer cans . . . there's enough stuff stuck to the floor to open a sperm bank!

JEFF: Let's take a ride up to the field.

SOOZE: Pony's coming. Just hold me for a minute.

(He does. They have a moment of peace)

I went by my sister's this afternoon.

JEFF: Yeah?

SOOZE: Jerry was outside lighting the barbecue and Debbie's in the kitchen making macaroni salad. I'm watching the baby in his crib and Jerry Junior was playing with his truck on the floor and I suddenly felt like I couldn't breathe.

JEFF: Because of the kids.

SOOZE: I don't know. They're great kids. I love them. I do. But it all seems so pathetic. And Debbie's my sister and she's like this stranger. She acts like I'm a kid. Like she's mature and I'm not. Like she knows something I don't.

JEFF: Because you're smart enough not to get married when you're two years out of high school.

SOOZE: I guess.

JEFF: Because you're smart enough not to get knocked-up two times in three years.

SOOZE: You're right.

JEFF: Don't compare yourself with your sister. You're completely different! You have a life. You're going to school. You're an artist, she's a housewife married to a guy who puts up aluminum siding.

(Pause. The embrace has broken)

SOOZE: I was talking to Mr. Brooks yesterday, he has this friend
in New York who wants to sublet his apartment. Six-fifty
a month.

JEFF: Yeah.

SOOZE: I could swing that, six-fifty.

JEFF: Sooze.

SOOZE: What?

JEFF: Did it ever occur to you that I might have some feelings
about you moving to New York?

SOOZE: What feelings?

JEFF: Us.

SOOZE: Of course!

JEFF: And?

SOOZE: Come with me!

JEFF: No! See that's not what I'm saying.

(Jeff walks away from Sooze)

SOOZE: Well, what are you saying?

JEFF: I could go to New York if I wanted. But what's the point?
So I can learn how to order a cappuccino? So I can get
mugged by some crackhead? So I can see homeless people up close?

SOOZE: So what do you want to do?

JEFF: Nothing.

SOOZE: No one does nothing, Jeff.

JEFF *(Defiant)*: I'm going to break new ground.

SOOZE: New ground? Taking one community college course on
the history of Nicaragua, while barely holding a job pack-
ing boxes?

JEFF: My job is not who I am. I don't need that.

SOOZE: What is it you need?

JEFF: Nothing. Too many possessions clutter your brain.

SOOZE: You find that in a fortune cookie?

JEFF: Tim said it.

SOOZE: Tim! Tim's an alcoholic. His brain is cluttered without possessions.

JEFF: Tim is honest. And I think that counts for something. I wish I were half as honest as he is. *(Pause)* Did you know that when Tim got out of the service, he hitchhiked from here to San Francisco and back?

SOOZE: Well, golly! Hitchhiker, Air Force dropout, corner bum, racist. My hero. He's just some guy hanging out. You act like he's God.

JEFF: Because he knows. Because he's been there.

SOOZE: He's a loser.

JEFF: And what am I?

SOOZE: Jeff, you're . . .

(Jeff walks away from her)

JEFF: All I want to do is make something that shatters the world. If I can't do that, I don't want to do anything.

SOOZE: That's egotistical.

JEFF: No it isn't! What's your goal? Status? Money? Getting your picture on the cover of some glossy magazine?

SOOZE: My goal is to make art.

JEFF: Why can't you do that here? What's wrong with here? How is something else better?

SOOZE: Why should I stay here, Jeff? So I can sit next to you and watch the lights change while you bitch about Burn-field? So we can talk about dead high-school teachers? So

I can spend the rest of my life guessing what it would be like to be a real artist? So you and I can *fuck* while your parents are out having dinner at The Sizzler? I mean, what are we doing? You and me?

JEFF: I don't know. I just want us to be happy. You got this thing about leaving, about New York. I want you to stay. I don't want you to go away. Who will I talk to? Who will I hang with? Who will I make love to?

SOOZE: Jeff.

JEFF: Who will I dream with?

SOOZE: You don't have any dreams.

(Buff enters from behind the store, fixing his fly, sees Sooze and Jeff arguing and freezes)

I'm getting beer.

(Sooze leaves. Jeff sits on the bench, inspecting his car keys. Buff goes to the pay phone, singing to himself, dials)

BUFF *(On the phone)*: Frankie!!! What you doing? Sleeping? Don't sleep! Sleep when you're dead, come on down the corner! . . . So put your clothes on and come down, man! I want to see you. And bring that weed you just bought! What? Fuck you, man! *(Hangs up. To Jeff)* So the old man let you have the Cherokee? Excellent. Maybe we'll do some off-roading later.

JEFF: I can't.

BUFF: Why the fuck not?

JEFF: He checks for mud on the tires when I bring it home.

BUFF: Shit. So we'll take Pony's stretch off-road.

JEFF: I seriously doubt Pony has a stretch.

BUFF: Bet you money he's in a stretch right now. Little color TV going. One of those mini-bars with scotch and shit in crystal bottles. Stacks of coke. A naked babe sitting on his lap stuffing a bong with highly resinous Hawaiian buds. Blow, babes, smoke. Can't wait till he gets here.

JEFF: You should have a checkup. You're delusional.

BUFF: He's a rock star, man. That's the rock star thing. Bet he has a babe with him right out of a triple-X video. *(Mimes a porno actress getting butt-fucked and growling with orgasmic pleasure)* Oh! Oh! Oh! Give it to me, Pony, you stud!

JEFF: Dream on.

(Jeff stands and walks away from Buff's antics)

BUFF *(Following)*: You wanna bet he's with a girl?

JEFF: He's not with a girl.

(Buff mimes giving head)

BUFF: Oh! Oh! Pony, it's so huge! Oh my God!

JEFF: He probably gets bored with all that shit.

BUFF: Oh yeah? How do you figure that?

JEFF: There's a limit to how much partying you can do.

(Bee-Bee enters, running her fingers through her hair, sprucing herself up. She sits on the bench)

BUFF: No there isn't.

JEFF: I'd get bored.

BUFF: I wouldn't. If I were in his shoes, every morning I'd get
up singing, man. Do my workout. Take a shower, followed
by a hearty breakfast of steak and eggs, washed down with
a pot of hot coffee and a six-pack of Bud Lite. Then I'd
smoke a joint and tell my bodyguard to go find my babe
who would appear decked out in her all-black-leather
Victoria's Secret custom-made bodysuit, so I'd like have to
chew all her clothes off until she was completely nude.
Except she'd have these amazing dragon tattoos all over
her body and pierced nipples with little gold peace signs
hanging off 'em. And then she'd pull out this half ounce
of blow and we'd snap out these mongo lines, vaporize a
few million brain cells, screw for about an hour, then
spend the rest of the morning trashed, watching *Gilligan's
Island.*

JEFF: Yeah, and what would you do in the afternoon?

BUFF: Same. More of the same. I'd just keep doing the same
thing all the time, around and around the clock with an
occasional burger or slice thrown in for vitamins and
energy. And instead of Gilligan, we'd watch Captain Kirk.

JEFF: Sounds depressing.

*(Buff, as he continues to talk, sits next to Bee-Bee and
casually puts his arm around her)*

BUFF: Come on, man, tell me you wouldn't love it!

JEFF: I'm not saying I wouldn't love it. I'm saying after awhile
it would wear thin.

BUFF: A long while. A long, long while. A long, long, long, long
while!

JEFF *(Acknowledging Buff's arm around Bee-Bee)*: What's this? Romance?

BUFF: We're exploring possibilities. You got any grass?

JEFF: No.

(Buff stands. Stretches)

BUFF: I've got this sudden urge to see Frankie. *(To Bee-Bee)* You comin'?

(Buff exits with Bee-Bee. Jeff is alone once more. He stands and goes off behind the dumpster to pee.

A guitar can be heard offstage, getting louder. It stops)

PONY *(Offstage)*: Sooze? JEFF?

(Jeff hears him, but since he's in the middle of his pee, can't stop.

A chunky, long-haired kid wearing round, wire-rimmed ultra-black sunglasses enters: Pony. He has an electric guitar slung onto his shoulder.

Jeff quickly zips up and comes around the store, face to face with Pony)

JEFF: Hey!

PONY *(Quietly)*: Hey, man.

JEFF: *Pony?*

(Jeff rushes up to Pony and embraces him)

PONY: Jeff! Wow.

JEFF: Pony!

(Pony breaks away and looks around)

PONY: You alone?

JEFF: No. Uh. Wanna beer?

PONY: Sure.

(Jeff passes a beer to Pony, takes one for himself, and they open them simultaneously. Pony looks out toward the audience and waves to someone. Jeff follows his look)

JEFF: That's your limo, huh?

PONY: The record company makes me use it. It's dumb, I know.

JEFF: Never been in one.

PONY: I'll give you a ride later. So you're just here alone?

JEFF: They just went. You know, to get refreshments.

PONY: Sooze?

JEFF: She's here. She'll be here.

PONY: You and her still . . . ?

JEFF: Yeah.

PONY: That's good. That's important. She's so great. *(Looks around)* Wow, man. "The Corner." Nothing's changed!

JEFF: You've only been gone a year. They give you a limo, huh?

PONY: Yeah. The driver knows Billy Joel. Wow, huh?

JEFF *(Weak laugh)*: Heh, that's funny. I saw your album at Musicland up the mall.

PONY: Yeah, we're starting to get good placement. We've sold over ninety thousand units. Danny says we're gonna get a gold record.

JEFF: Gold record, huh? Must be great. Living the wild life, huh?

PONY: No. . . .

JEFF: Rock star. Fame. Fortune. Sex.

PONY: It's hard work. The road, man. The road is hell. Airport-hotel-show-airport-hotel-show-airport-hotel-show.   Still living at your mom's?

JEFF: I just crash there. Alot of nights I'm just out. You know.

PONY: Yeah, I saw your Dad's Cherokee parked out front so I knew you were here.

(Erica enters, talking on a cell phone; a dark beauty, with sophisticated hair and makeup, sporting a tight sweater, bell bottoms, boots and a "day-runner")

ERICA: Uh-huh, uh-huh, uh-huh. OK. Cool. *(Hangs up phone)* He says "eight AM" *(Finds a seat on the bench and makes a note in her day-runner)*

PONY: Great! Erica, Jeff, Jeff, Erica.

(Erica and Jeff, unsure of their relative status, nod toward one another)

JEFF: Hi.

ERICA: Hi.

JEFF *(Off of Erica)*: So you having any fun, man?

PONY: Some. People are weird, they think you're somebody special if they see you on MTV. You know?

JEFF: Yeah, when you're really just nobody.

PONY: Not "nobody."

JEFF: I mean, just a person.

PONY: It's amazing to be back home. I mean we've been playing big places everywhere but when we did the sound
check at the stadium it suddenly hit me. Twenty thousand
people, you know? I mean last time I played around here
was the prom! *(Laughs)*

JEFF *(Uncomfortable)*: Yeah. The prom. Heh.

PONY: I thought you guys might come to the show . . .

JEFF: Sooze screwed up the tickets, you know?

PONY: We were pretty good tonight.

ERICA: You were *amazing* tonight.

PONY: We were?

ERICA: Oh yeah!

PONY *(To Jeff)*: So what's happening with you? How's college?

JEFF: I dropped out. I mean, this semester I'm just taking a
class three nights a week. I'm trying to rethink my value
system. You know?

*(Pony nods sagely. Jeff looks to Erica for some kind of
response. She smiles, pleasant and vacant)*

I'm more writing stuff. Short pieces.

ERICA: I love writing. Anne Rice. I love Anne Rice.

PONY: Pieces, huh? You should try writing songs.

JEFF: I've thought of that, actually.

PONY: I mean it. You're a good writer. I remember those things
you'd write for Mister Fresher. Funny shit. *(To Erica)* He
wrote this thing about his dick once. Read it in front of the
whole class.

ERICA: Oh, I'd love to read that!

JEFF: But so, you think I should?

PONY: What?

JEFF: Write? Because I have. Written some things. You know.

PONY: Songs?

JEFF: They could be songs.

PONY: Yeah? You should show 'em to me.

JEFF: No.

PONY: Really.

JEFF: Now?

PONY: Maybe later.

(Beat)

JEFF *(Relaxing, smiles)*: Hey.

PONY: Hey, you know?

JEFF *(Chatty)*: I'm thinking, he's out there, he's touring, he's a big deal now. MTV. Stadiums. And then you show up and you're just Pony.

PONY: I'm just Pony, man.

JEFF: Now that I'm thinking about it, it *would* be interesting to do something together.

PONY: It would.

JEFF: Yeah. *(Suddenly serious)* You're doing good work, man. You're inspirational.

PONY *(Serious)*: So are you, man.

JEFF: Maybe I'll stop by the house and get the songs later.

PONY: You should.

(Sooze enters, hauling bags of beer, pissed off)

SOOZE: Didn't want to serve me! Made me show him an I.D.! I said, "I'm not showing you any fucking I.D. You know me, I'm in here every other night!" Fucking long-haired, pot-

bellied forty-something baby-boomer dick-wit. Went to a
protest march, dropped acid and saw God.

JEFF: Sooze.

(Jeff gets Sooze's attention onto the new arrival)

SOOZE: PONY! HI! *(Runs up to him and gives him a heartfelt
hug)* Oh my God. You showed up. Oh, shit! There's your
limo! Wow, a real limo. I never saw a black one before.

PONY: It's stupid isn't it?

SOOZE: No, it isn't . . . it's . . . cool.

PONY: You look good, Sooze. Like your head's in a good place.
(Pause) Still doing your painting?

SOOZE: Sometimes. I'm starting to do performances. And I
don't look good, I look like shit. My head's in a shitty
place.

PONY: Performances?

SOOZE: Performance art. You know. Laurie Anderson? Karen
Finley? Henry Rollins?

PONY: Oh, yeah. Sure. I met Sandra Bernhardt in L.A.

SOOZE: You did? She's alright.

PONY: She's incredible in person. My manager, Danny, took me
to this restaurant and there she was.

SOOZE: Wow. She was just sitting there?

PONY: Oh yeah. Just sitting there eating a salad. That kind of
thing happens all the time in L.A. I've met Johnny Depp.

JEFF: Johnny Depp?

PONY: You'd like him.

JEFF: No, I wouldn't.

SOOZE: Jeff, how do you know if you would like somebody or
not?

PONY: He seemed like a great guy.

(As the tension builds between Jeff and Sooze, Jeff sits on the downstage curb and distances himself from the conversation)

SOOZE: I'm thinking of moving to New York. To school. And paint. Performances, paint.

PONY: New York, huh?

SOOZE: Not a good move, huh?

PONY: I think it's a great move. You have to go. You always did such great work. I still have some of those drawings you'd do in study hall.

SOOZE: You do?

(Sooze glances at Jeff)

PONY: Sure. Jeff, don't you think Sooze should go to New York?

JEFF: It would depend. But, yeah, she should. Sure. I think Sooze should . . .

(Buff rushes in, breathless, crosses the stage and ducks behind the corner of the building. Bee-Bee follows right after, laughing)

BUFF: If the cops roll by, I'm not here!

(Tim hangs over the edge of the roof)

TIM: What happened?

(Buff cowers behind the dumpster)

BEE-BEE: Nothing happened. Frankie's mom called the cops
'cause Buff was climbing up the drainpipe trying to get to
Frankie's room, so he could get some pot.

TIM: Did you get it?

*(Tim hops down to join Buff. Buff triumphantly pulls out a
small baggie of grass)*

BUFF: He put up a struggle, but the forces of good won out in
the end.

(Buff spies Pony)

HEY! Pony, man! Great concert tonight!

PONY: You were there?

BUFF: No, but I heard it was great.

SOOZE: Pony, this is my friend, Bee-Bee.

PONY: Hey. How's it going?

(Everyone looks at Bee-Bee. She's tongue-tied)

BEE-BEE: Hi.

BUFF: So tell us, man! Blow. Party-time. Trashing hotel rooms.
Babes around the clock.

PONY: We don't have the time for that.

(Buff notices Erica sitting on the bench for the first time)

BUFF: What about her?

PONY: Erica? Erica's the publicist for the band.

BUFF: Yeah, right. "Publicist."

PONY: She works for the record company. She takes care of interviews, shit like that. I was just doing an interview and Erica said she'd like to see Burnfield.

(Jeff is getting restless)

JEFF: What are we doing?

(Jeff's question goes unanswered)

BUFF *(To Erica)*: We're old friends of Pony's. We all go way back. To our childhood.

ERICA: He's told me. Burnfield. We all hear about Burnfield.

JEFF: What does he tell you? About how we started the band? The "early days."

ERICA: Oh, you were in the band?

JEFF: I helped start it.

PONY: Well, not exactly, Jeff.

JEFF: Well, for awhile . . .

PONY: You came by one day and played harmonica. But that was before we were really a band. We were just kids fooling around.

JEFF: I came by more than once.

(Tim has kept to himself up to now, drinking and smoking joints with Buff. Now he rouses and enters the conversation)

TIM: Danny? Who's Danny?

SOOZE: Danny David, their manager.

TIM: "Danny David," what is that, a Jewish name? I knew a Jew in the Force. Pilot. Came from Shaker Heights, Ohio. Big nose. Always talking. Funny guy. Is Danny one of those funny kind of Jews, Pony?

PONY: I don't know.

TIM: You don't know? You don't know if he's funny or not?

ERICA: He talks alot. He's funny.

(Tim turns his focus on Erica. He sits next to her on the bench and blithely puts his arm around her shoulder)

TIM: So, you came by to see how the other half lives, eh? Well, here we are, what do you think?

(Erica smiles, as if this is meant as a joke)

Pretty pathetic, huh? Kind of like a documentary on educational TV.

ERICA: I think it's nice here. It's different.

(Tim turns to Pony)

TIM: What do they interview you about?

PONY: There's this benefit for Somalia we're going to do. And you know . . . my work . . .

TIM: Your "work?" What do you tell them about "your work?"

PONY: I explain what my songs are about, you know. The message: "Find honesty, tear down the walls, reach out to another naked human being, help the revolution." How I write it, get my ideas, you know.

TIM: How *do* you get your ideas?

SOOZE: Leave him alone Tim.

TIM: I want to know! I'm curious. How do you get your ideas?

(Pony smiles)

SOOZE: Tim's jealous. He wants to have ideas too.

TIM: Yeah, I'm jealous. I'm jealous of Jew-loving faggots who do benefits for starving niggers.

(Tim sits with his back to the wall and closes his eyes. Pause. Sooze looks at Jeff)

SOOZE: Jeff.

JEFF: What?

(Tim's motionless. Bee-Bee smokes by herself. Pony, feeling a bit confused, strums his guitar by himself. Buff has fixed onto Erica. As she walks over to Tim to say something, Buff stops her and asks:)

BUFF: You're not his publicist.

ERICA: Sure I am. It's fun. You meet the best people. Help them do their thing. Get the word out. Widen the demographic.

BUFF: And you're, like, what else?

ERICA: Am I sleeping with him?

BUFF: That's one way of putting it.

ERICA: Am I *fucking* him?

BUFF: Shit.

ERICA: Pony, what would you say our relationship is?

PONY *(Considers, then)*: Mother-daughter.

ERICA: Pony and I are "friends."

BUFF: So like, you're available?

ERICA *(Amused, glances at Pony)*: In what way?

BUFF: In a horizontal and wet way.

SOOZE: Can we stop this, Buff?

TIM *(Eyes still closed)*: He's simply having verbal intercourse, Sooze.

SOOZE: No, he's not, he's objectifying her. He's entertaining us at her expense.

ERICA: It's OK. He's . . . what's your name?

BUFF: Buff.

ERICA: "Buff" is funny.

TIM: She likes Buff. She thinks Buff's funny. So why don't you keep your feminist hole closed?

SOOZE: Why don't you swallow your cock and choke on it? Oh, I forgot, it's not big enough.

TIM: Cunt . . .

JEFF: Tim . . .

TIM *(Opens his eyes, starts to stand)*: You fucking faggot, what are you going to say?

SOOZE *(To Jeff)*: It's OK. Forget it.

TIM *(Drunk)*: Excuse me, I was speaking to the faggot.

JEFF *(Changing the subject)*: So Pony, where are you staying? Your mother's house?

(Tim sits back and closes his eyes)

TIM *(Grumbling to himself)*: Fucking faggot.

PONY: No, that can be kind of a hassle. I stay at the Four Seasons. It's easier.

(Tim shouts with incongruous inanity)

TIM: "I STAY AT THE FOUR SEASONS. IT'S EASIER."

(Tim gets up and walks off toward the liquor store. He smiles toward Erica on his way out. She smiles back)

JEFF: The Four Seasons? Really? I hear it's nice there.
PONY: Hey, it's a bed and hot water, you know?

(Pony smiles at Sooze)

SOOZE: What are you doing next? I mean, what does the band do now?
PONY: We go back in the studio. New album.
BUFF: Need any help?

(Laughs. Pony looks at Buff deeply)

I could do the video. I make videos now, man.
PONY: You ready to move to Los Angeles? We're going to be making a new video. You have a reel?
BUFF: Reel?
PONY: Like something I can see?
BUFF: Sure.
PONY: Then, you never know. And I was thinking, Sooze, you could do our next cover.
SOOZE: You don't want me to do your cover.
PONY: I don't want you to do the cover, I *need* you to do the cover.

SOOZE: You're not serious.

PONY: I'm always serious.

SOOZE: They would never let me do what I want.

PONY: I get final approval. It's in my contract.

SOOZE: Would I get paid?

PONY: We'd have to fly you out. For meetings.

SOOZE: Yeah?

PONY: Yeah.

SOOZE *(Embarrassed by how delighted she is)*: That would
be . . . that would be something I would want to do.

PONY: Good. *(Puts his beer down, stretches and stands)* You
know something? I feel good. I feel good because I'm
hanging out with you guys. I forgot what it was like to just
hang out. And you know why it's so good? Because you
guys are real, you guys have a sense of humor, you live
your lives. The guys on the road, the band, all they think
about is scoring chicks. And Danny, all he talks about is
money.

BUFF: Yeah, we're above all that.

PONY: No, I mean, when we were driving out here, I told,
George, the driver, to roll the windows down, just so I
could smell the air. The smell of freshly cut grass . . . great!
I could see into the picture windows of the houses. Fami-
lies watching TV, eating dinner, guys drinking beer. It's
the suburbs! They don't call it the "American Dream" for
nothing.

*(Pony takes a break from his rhapsody and receives blank
stares)*

JEFF: Who's they?

PONY: This afternoon I went by the old mall and just walked around by myself. I just wanted to be alone and get, you know, that old mall feeling.

SOOZE: What's that?

(Pony strums his guitar idly)

PONY: You know, safety, security. I've been trying to write something about this. But it's new. . . . Na . . . never mind.

BUFF: Come on, play it, man!

SOOZE: Play it!

(Pony relents, starts to play)

PONY: OK. Uh . . .

(Buff and Sooze find a seat on the ground)

BUFF: Free concert!!!

(Pony starts the song tentatively, then finds his voice)

PONY:

    I get up in the morning and I go to work
    I have a car . . . lawn and a TV, my boss is a jerk
    My kids are good, my wife is sane
    When I wake up tomorrow gonna do it all again . . .

    I drove down the highway there was a big jam
    A family had died inside their mini-van
    There was a back-up, you know it went for miles
    But as bad as it was, it was gone after awhile . . .

(Chorus)
You may think there's nothing to it, and
The truth is hard to see
To be a man invisible is a remarkable
Thing to be
Thing to be. Thing to be. Thing to be.

BUFF: I'm glad you put TV in your song, man. That's
important.

JEFF: So who are you?

PONY: What?

JEFF: I mean, if we're like "the man invisible," what are you?

PONY: I'm . . . an artist. You know, there's life and then there's
the artist watching the life, commenting on it.

JEFF: That's what I do, too.

PONY: What?

JEFF: Comment. Say things. Think. Whatever. Why are you so
special?

PONY: Well, it's one thing to think. It's another thing to communicate it to people. I'm doing that with my music. "If a
tree falls in the forest and no one's there to hear it, does it
make a sound?"

(Pony has been answering Jeff by speaking to Sooze)

JEFF: Of course it does!

SOOZE: That's my worst fear. Making a sound and no one
hears it.

*(Pony and Sooze are having a conversation, oblivious to
Jeff)*

PONY: Mine too.

BUFF: Wait. What happened to the tree?

JEFF: Hold on a second!

PONY: You know what I'm saying?

SOOZE: Sure, you make art, you want people to see it.

(Jeff has found himself standing over Sooze and Pony, who are locked in their own conversation. He interjects)

JEFF: Yeah, sure. But that doesn't mean your tree is not artistic if no one cuts it down.

SOOZE: Jeff likes to argue for the sake of arguing.

JEFF: No, I don't.

SOOZE: Yes, you do.

JEFF: I don't.

SOOZE: You do.

JEFF *(Walking away)*: No. I don't.

(Conversation has stopped for a moment. Buff is still focused on Erica)

BUFF: You come from, like a town like this?

ERICA: Sort of. I come from an "area."

BUFF: Oh. Cool. Not "South Central?"

ERICA: No. Not South Central.

(Tim has reentered over the last two lines, a fresh six-pack under his arm, sipping a king-size. He finds his favorite spot and sits, pops a beer)

TIM: What area?

ERICA: Hmmmmm?

TIM: Not South Central. Where?

ERICA: Bel Air.

TIM *(Pause)*: You rich?

ERICA: Not really. Middle class.

TIM: Me too. Middle class.

ERICA: Maybe upper middle class.

TIM: Yeah. So your Dad's a big deal, huh?

ERICA: He thinks so. No, he is.

(Erica's a little embarrassed by having this focus on her. She's found herself standing in the middle of the area. She smiles over to Pony, who is now seated by Sooze. Tim stands and approaches her)

TIM: You love him alot, he bought you a BMW for your birth-day but finally you had to move out and get your own place.

(Erica doesn't say anything as Tim holds a hand over her head and shuts his eyes, speaks like a mind reader)

Your parents hate your smoking. You didn't tell them about the abortion. You know your Dad's having an affair with someone at work. You used to be bulimic, but now you're over it. You subscribe to *Vanity Fair*. You have a personal trainer. You've been seeing the same therapist for years. You have your nails done by a professional.

BUFF *(To Jeff)*: What's he doing, man?

TIM: You Jewish?

ERICA: My Dad. Not my Mom. I know. You hate Jews.

TIM: I never said that. I just like to know who I'm dealing with.

(Erica walks away from him)

ERICA *(Cold)*: Now you know who you're dealing with. What are you going to do about it?

(While this conversation goes on, Bee-Bee gets up and exits, taking the boom box with her. No one notices.

Jeff is in a funk. Tim is drinking. Pony, sitting on the curb, starts to sing and strum, serenading Sooze)

PONY:

I know it's not easy
To open your eyes
See what's around you
Listen to their lies

They are old
We are young
They are fat
We are fun
They're asleep

We are new
They will die
I love you

I sound like an idiot
Watching the parade

I know there's no tomorrow
Only the charade

I am dead
Deep inside
In my head
All the lies
There's no then
Only now
I will love
Show me how

(Chorus)
I burnt my hand in a fire
Haven't slept for a week
Cut my feet on the glass
Never finding what I seek
I need salvation
I need salvation
I need salvation
Kiss my wounds . . .

(Sooze is impressed. She smiles at Pony. Jeff suddenly kicks the trash can over and stands)

JEFF: Hey! Pony!

PONY: Huh?

JEFF: If we wanted to hear you sing, we would have gone to your concert.

SOOZE: What a nice thing to say, Jeff.

JEFF: You ride in here like fucking God! You're a big deal! You've been everywhere, you know everything. Fuck you!

PONY: I didn't say I know everything.

JEFF: Well, you don't.

(Jeff blurs in his thinking. Runs out of things to say. Kicks the trash can again)

SOOZE: Jeff!

JEFF: So you sold ninety thousand units. So what? Is that supposed to mean you're a genius, an artist? You're higher up the ladder? You got an extra gold star on your forehead?

TIM: Jeff, you're cute when you're angry.

JEFF: You know what I'm saying. Why don't you write a song about having dinner with Johnny Depp?

PONY: What are you saying, Jeff? You don't like my stuff, I won't sing it. Sorry.

JEFF *(Loses his energy)*: That's not it. I'm saying . . . I'm saying . . . I don't need a limo to know who I am. OK?

TIM: OK! Right on!

JEFF *(Quietly)*: I know that I *don't* know. I know that much. I know that things are fucked up beyond belief and I know I have nothing original to say about any of it. I don't have an answer, I don't have a "message."

(Pause)

TIM: He isn't crying, is he?

JEFF: Shut up, Tim, it's not funny!

TIM: I think it is.

PONY: Jeff, now listen . . .

(Jeff swings wildly at Pony, ends up falling down)

BUFF *(Cheery)*: Hey, man, chill!

(Buff hands Jeff a beer. Jeff looks at the beer like he's never seen one before)

JEFF: "Man invisible."

PONY: Hey, man, I'm sorry if I said something wrong.

JEFF: It's OK. It's not you. It's this sidewalk. This cell. This void. You know?

PONY: No, look, I come here and I'm so used to everyone kissing my ass I think I'm a fucking star and I'm sorry if I'm full of attitude.

(Pony is diplomatic. Puts his arm around Jeff. Jeff crumbles)

JEFF: It's not you. It's not anybody. It's me.

PONY: Hey, man, it's OK!

JEFF: I have no brain. No eyes. The blind leading the blind. FUCK!

PONY: No, look, uh. Why don't we get something to eat? George can drive us, there's plenty of room in the stretch.

(Pony locks eyes with Sooze as he massages Jeff's shoulders)

SOOZE: Chinese. Hung Suk take-out is open till one.

JEFF: Go pick something up and bring it back here.

PONY: Sure. But come with us, man. I said I would give you a ride in the limo. You too, Buff! Tim!

BUFF: Def.

TIM: Don't ride in limos. I'll wait here and guard the sidewalk.

(Sooze comes over to Jeff and holds his lapels)

SOOZE: Come on.

JEFF: Go ahead.

SOOZE: I'm not going if you don't come.

BUFF: Come on, man. You can hang me out the window! I'll do tricks. I'll puke on people for you.

(Jeff laughs)

JEFF: I don't feel like it. That's all.

SOOZE: Why don't you just try? *(An afterthought)* Where's Bee-Bee?

(Jeff stands and they all start walking, except Erica, who stays where she is. Watching Tim. Sooze and Jeff exit)

PONY: You coming, Erica?

SOOZE *(Offstage)*: Bee-Bee! Where'd you go?

(Something about the way Erica looks at him sends Pony a silent signal)

PONY: Oh, OK.

(Pony, Sooze and Jeff move off, leaving Buff standing and watching Erica)

BUFF: You sure?

(But Erica is turned away, stubbing out a cigarette, and— pretends?—she doesn't hear him)

JEFF *(Offstage)*: BUFF!

(Buff gives it up and leaves.
Erica lights a cigarette. She's on the bench, Tim's on his spot, drinking)

ERICA: Well, you got everything right but the car. My dad didn't get me a BMW, it was a Porsche. *(Pause)* You seem to know alot about me, I don't know anything about you. What kind of music you like?

TIM: Military marching bands.

(She laughs. He tilts his beer back, finishes it off and throws the can off)

ERICA: You know where Bel Air is, don't you? You know what it is.

TIM: I saw it once on TV.

ERICA: You think I'm rich and you hate me.

TIM: Don't tell me what I think. You don't know me.

ERICA: If I don't, I want to.

TIM: No, you don't.

ERICA: You were in the army?

(Tim drinks and then starts talking)

TIM: United States Air Force. Biggest mistake of my life.
ERICA: Were you a pilot?
TIM: Oh yeah, me and Tom Cruise.

(Erica comes down to Tim and sits by him)

ERICA: What was it like?
TIM: I was a dopey kid mopping floors and kissing officer ass. Enlisted out of high school. What did I know about officer training school or having a college degree or coming from the right family? "It's not a job, it's an adventure." I hated it. I had to get out, so I copped kitchen duty, chopped off the tip of my little finger and three days later I was a free man.

(Tim takes a drink)

ERICA: You cut off your little finger?!
TIM: They sewed it back on.
ERICA: Let me see!

(Tim puts his little finger in the air. She grabs his hand and holds it as he speaks)

TIM: Honorable discharge. Disabled while serving. I get a check every month.

(Uncomfortable, Tim takes his hand back)

ERICA: I guess you get some kind of experience from it.
TIM: Oh yeah. I'm much smarter now. I got taught.
ERICA: A lesson?
TIM: "A lesson?" A big lesson. Shut up and stay where you belong. Learn your place or lose your place.
ERICA: And not so happy?

(Tim smiles weakly at her)

TIM: Happy? That's your game. I pass.
ERICA: I'm not so happy. Go to the gym. Eat the yogurt. Go to the gym. Check the voice-mail. Smoke the low-tar cigarette. Shave the bikini line. Most of the time I don't feel anything, just a mild expectation. Like, "Maybe somebody interesting will be backstage after the show tonight." I guess I'm hoping for the unexpected.

(Erica and Tim's eyes meet. It holds for a second before Tim looks back down)

You know, Pony told me about his friends in Burnfield but frankly from what he said I figured you were just a bunch of kids. I really came out here for the pizza. He told me it was incredible.
TIM *(Confused, shy)*: It is.
ERICA: No, but I mean underneath all the noise you're really a nice man. You're intense but you're sweet. Aren't you?

(Tim stands up quickly and walks away from her)

TIM: What was your name?

ERICA: Erica.

TIM: You think you and I are alike, Erica?

ERICA *(Thinks)*: Deep down. Way down.

TIM: It's a mistake to think that.

ERICA: We can still talk. It's nice to talk.

TIM: It's "nice" to do alot of things.

ERICA: That's what I mean.

TIM: You don't understand me. What I'm saying here.

ERICA *(Seductive)*: I want to understand.

TIM: I'm not a "nice man." I'm not "sweet."

ERICA: I know.

TIM: Oh yeah?

ERICA: Yeah. Hey, I'm a big girl. If I didn't want to be here, I'd be in a limo right now with a bunch of kids. Looking for Chinese food.

(Tim looks at her. There is fear in his eyes)

TIM: You don't know.

ERICA: No?

TIM: No.

(Erica is right up to him now, hands behind her back, offering herself to him)

ERICA *(Cold and clear)*: So teach me a lesson.

(Tim kisses her. The kissing becomes animated, strenuous, awkward. Tim is aggressive, but then Erica returns the aggression, reaches for his crotch, rubs him. Tim breaks away)

TIM: Whoaaa . . . *(Looks her in the eyes)* You sure about this?

(Erica nods her head, as if to say: "I am yours." Tim takes her by the hand and leads her off. Music comes up as lights dim)

ACT
THREE

The storefront is shuttered.

Bee-Bee sits with her back to the wall smoking a cigarette, Buff's boom box next to her, playing music. An uncracked quart bottle of Jack Daniels sits before her. She watches the bottle as if it were something alive, about to speak to her.

Tim is curled up asleep at the other end of the wall, oblivious.

Jeff enters. He sees Bee-Bee and the bottle, notes Tim sleeping and then snaps off the radio.

JEFF: I just walked all the way from the Center to here.

(Bee-Bee doesn't answer)

I haven't walked that far since Junior High.

(Still no answer. Jeff doesn't care. He's imbued with some strange new energy)

You know you missed the big limo ride. We were looking for you.

(She stubs out her cigarette)

BEE-BEE: How was it?

JEFF: Disgusting. And stupid. I got out. *(Tries to rouse Tim)* Tim! Get up!

(Tim doesn't stir. Jeff notices the bottle of booze)

I thought you didn't drink.

BEE-BEE: I don't. Anymore.

JEFF: Uh-huh. Can I have some?

BEE-BEE: I don't care. Knock yourself out.

(Jeff takes the bottle, uncaps it and takes a swig)

JEFF: Tim!

(Motionless, Tim could be dead. Jeff takes another swig)

It's weird how things can change. One minute everything is fucked, and then, you look at it from a different angle and it all makes sense. People used to walk alot more than they do now, and you know, I don't think they worried about things half as much. I walked for twenty minutes and everything suddenly became clear. You know?

BEE-BEE: Oh yeah.

JEFF: Ever hear the saying: "This too shall pass?"

BEE-BEE: Sure, all the time. In group.

JEFF: Group?

BEE-BEE: Rehab. Outpatient. I have to go once a week. It's kinda like A.A.

JEFF: Oh yeah, you had to go to Highgate. You stole a car or something.

BEE-BEE: Or something.

JEFF: How long were you in there?

BEE-BEE: Ninety days. But now I just go once a week. I'm rehabilitated, see?

(Jeff swigs from the bottle)

JEFF: You shouldn't drink, then. Are you gonna drink?

BEE-BEE: No. Yes. Maybe. Fuck.

JEFF: That would suck if you had to go back . . . to rehab.

BEE-BEE: It would suck big time. I'd kill myself first.

JEFF: Is it really bad?

BEE-BEE: It was hell with windows. So noisy, I always had a headache. Smelly. Shit on the walls. There were kids my age sucking their thumbs, wetting their pants. Most of us were there because of drugs, but you wanna know something funny? There were more drugs inside that fucking place than I ever saw on the outside. A kid from my floor shot up cough medicine, had convulsions right in front of me.

JEFF: Fuck.

BEE-BEE: Every day I woke up in my cell and I thought to myself, my parents put me here. Why? Because I stayed out all night one time. Because I broke the VCR when I was drunk. Because I was "out of control." I thought my parents loved me.

JEFF: They were trying to help.

BEE-BEE: Yeah. That's one way of looking at it.

JEFF: So now you don't drink?

BEE-BEE: I'm rehabilitated. I'm a productive member of society. I can *deal*—"one day at a fucking time."

(Bee-Bee pulls out a cigarette for Jeff and lights it for him. They sit smoking)

JEFF: You're pissed off at Buff. But Buff's a riot. He can be funny as shit.

BEE-BEE: Yeah.

JEFF: Sex is a weird thing. I mean when you think about it, we're just like these organisms with bizarre tentacles and orifices kind of poking and pushing into each other.

BEE-BEE: I don't know.

(Jeff drinks the whiskey)

JEFF: I was pretty down before too. But we were riding around and everyone's getting all excited and suddenly it just hit me what we were doing. We're getting off on the fact that we're in a car five feet longer than the rest. I got out and just started walking.

BEE-BEE: Yeah?

JEFF: Well, what it was—I didn't want to admit it, but I was jealous of Pony.

BEE-BEE: Sure. He's rich and famous, he's got everything and you've got nothing.

(Jeff doesn't expect Bee-Bee's blunt insight. He digests this and continues)

JEFF: But I mean, when I was walking I realized, he's stuck in that limo all the time, he's stuck with the autographs and the interviews. He has to do what his manager tells him to do. He isn't free. He's just part of the machine. And freedom's really all there is.

BEE-BEE: I guess.

JEFF: It used to scare me that I didn't know what was coming in my life. I always thought, what if I make the wrong move? You know? But maybe there isn't any right move. You know I was trying to figure it all out. But maybe you can't.

(Bee-Bee doesn't answer. Jeff stands up, slightly drunk)

Look at us. We all dress the same, we all talk the same, we all watch the same TV. No one's really different, even if they think they're different. "Oh boy, look at my tattoo!" You know?

(Bee-Bee has no expression on her face. She's very down, but as Jeff gets drunker, he doesn't notice)

And that makes me free, because I can do anything if I really don't care what the result is. I don't need money. I don't even need a future. I could knock out all my teeth with a hammer, so what? I could poke my eyes out. I'd still be alive. Strip naked and fart in the wind. At least I would know I was doing something real for two or three seconds. It's all about fear. And I'm not afraid anymore. Fuck it!

(Jeff starts disrobing. Bee-Bee watches him flatly. She absent-mindedly takes the bottle and drinks)

Because anything is possible. It is night on the planet earth and I am alive and someday I will be dead. Someday, I'll be bones in a box. But right now, I'm not. And anything is possible. And that's why I can go to New York with Sooze. Because each moment can be what it is. I'm on the train going there, I'm living there, I'm reading a newspaper, I'm walking down the street. There is no failure, there is no mistake. I just go and live there and what happens, happens. *(Down to his underwear)* So at this moment, I am getting naked. And I am not afraid. FUCK FEAR! FUCK MONEY! I WILL GO TO NEW YORK AND I WILL LIVE IN A BOX. I WILL SING WITH THE BUMS, I WILL STARVE BUT I WILL NOT DIE. I WILL LIVE. I WILL TALK TO GOD!

(Jeff swigs from the bottle of whiskey. He and Bee-Bee haven't seen Norman entering. Norman leans against a wall and casually lights a cigarette. Jeff starts to pull his underwear off, sees Norman and STOPS DEAD in his tracks. Instinctively, he reaches for his pants)

NORMAN: Don't you guys ever go home?

JEFF: What's your fucking problem?

NORMAN: What's yours?

JEFF: You fucking scared me, man!

NORMAN: My sister wanted me to check the store. She's afraid you and your friends are going to break the windows.

JEFF: That's stupid.

NORMAN: You're standing in the middle of the street with your penis sticking out and you're calling my sister stupid?

(Jeff grabs more clothes and starts to dress)

JEFF: Tim, look who's here. Hadji.

(Jeff nudges Tim with his foot, gets no reaction. He continues to dress. Norman disdainfully walks around them, examining the mess they've made and, finally, Tim lying on the ground. Through all of this, Bee-Bee sits motionless, smoking, looking at the ground)

NORMAN: We had a servant in Karachi who took to drinking. She died a beggar.

JEFF: Just because I'm having a couple of shots of Jack Daniels doesn't mean I'm an alcoholic.

NORMAN: Uh-huh.

JEFF: Besides, how could you have had a servant? You were poor.

NORMAN: We were not poor. In fact, some cousins of mine are very wealthy. And also in fact at one point we had a cook, a gardener, and I had a personal tutor. How do you think I learned to speak English so well? Or do you ever think about anything?

JEFF: So why did you come here if you had it so fucking great?

(Tim stirs. Norman stubs out his cigarette. He picks up a piece of garbage and throws it into the dumpster. Jeff is lacing up his shoes)

NORMAN: We used to have a shop in Southhall. That's in London . . . England.

JEFF: I know where London is.

NORMAN: Lots of trouble from the blacks. They would come in stealing things. I would argue with them. Then they came one night and burnt our shop to the ground. I thought it would be different here.

JEFF: We're not like them.

(Norman wipes his hand with a handkerchief as he approaches Jeff)

NORMAN: Let me give you some advice. You seem like a smart guy. This is not for you. This, what you are doing with your life. You know?

(Jeff gets to his feet and walks away from Norman)

JEFF: Thanks for the advice, but you wouldn't understand what's going on with me.

NORMAN: Very complicated.

JEFF: That's right.

NORMAN: Complicated or not, life moves on, eh? *(Looks at Bee-Bee, sitting off by herself)* Is she alright?

JEFF: Everyone's fine. We're all fine.

NORMAN: Well, if you're all so fine, why don't you all go home? And take him with you, otherwise I might sweep him up in the morning with the trash.

(Norman walks off. Jeff and Bee-Bee say nothing for a few seconds. Jeff nudges Tim again)

JEFF: Tim!

(Nothing. Pause)

BEE-BEE: Jeff?

JEFF: Yeah?

BEE-BEE: Nothin'.

JEFF: What?

BEE-BEE: Do you . . . do you ever get up in the morning and think: "Well, here's another day, just like the last one?" You know? Like what difference does it make? The days just keep coming, one after another . . . so . . .

JEFF *(Interrupting)*: I think that sometimes.

BEE-BEE: But I mean, if you lived them or not, what difference would it make, you know?

(Jeff moves toward Tim again)

JEFF: Tim, come on! Get up!

(Sooze and Pony enter carrying bags of Chinese food and two six-packs. Jeff greets them with cheer)

Food! I thought you guys got lost.

SOOZE: We took the scenic route past the high school. You would have enjoyed it.

(Jeff picks up a carton of fried rice. Through this interchange, Pony simply takes out food and eats, observing. To Bee-Bee:)

Where did you go?

BEE-BEE: Home.

SOOZE: Something wrong?

BEE-BEE: Nah . . . you know.

SOOZE: Where'd you go, Jeff?

JEFF: I got sick of listening to that demo tape over and over. I felt like a groupie.

SOOZE: I enjoyed the ride. I'm sorry you didn't.

JEFF: Wait a second . . . I don't want to fight. Listen, I'm sorry . . .

SOOZE: What?!

JEFF: I'm sorry. I mean it. When I got out of the limo I walked all the way from the Center to here and I figured something out.

(Sooze walks away, eating)

SOOZE: Oh yeah?

BUFF *(Offstage, shout-singing a drunken lyric)*:
JUMP AROUND! JUMP AROUND!
JUMP UP, JUMP UP AND GET DOWN!

(Buff comes bounding in, continues to sing the song, ad nauseam. As he does, he hops around, getting in Jeff's face)

JUMP AROUND! JUMP AROUND!
JUMP UP, JUMP UP AND GET DOWN!

(Buff bounces through the group, toward the back wall. He crashes into the wall and falls down)

SOOZE: He threw up out the window of the limo.

(Buff gets up, brushes himself off, no visible damage. He veers toward the food.

Through all of this, Tim, without anyone noticing, steals the Jack Daniels, hoists himself onto the dumpster, then on up to the roof.

Buff scoops up a pint of fried rice and eats with relish. He talks as he eats, spitting rice)

BUFF: When I'm shitfaced, I get this huge appetite. I love to eat. Don't know why. Most people don't but I do.

(All watch with amazement as Buff sucks down the entire pint of rice. He gives a satisfied look all around. Then:)

Oh shit! *(Runs out to the curb and starts puking his guts out. Then he rolls onto his back, groaning)* Oh, wow, I don't feel good.

SOOZE: He should go home.

PONY: I don't think George'll let him into the limo like that. He already had to clean down the side.

JEFF: I'll take him.

SOOZE: You sure?

BUFF: Ohhhhhh!

(Jeff helps Buff onto his feet. He turns to Sooze)

JEFF: You coming?

SOOZE: The food . . . I didn't eat at my sister's.

JEFF: Never mind, I'll be right back.

(Jeff exits with Buff)

BUFF *(Exiting)*: Shit. I probably shouldn't have eaten that.

(Pony starts laughing as Sooze picks up some food)

PONY: Burnfield! There's no place like it.

SOOZE: Burnfield: pizza and puke capital of the world.

PONY: I can't believe you're still here.

SOOZE: I'm moving to New York.

PONY: If . . .

SOOZE: No, I'm going. Soon.

PONY: Uh-huh.

SOOZE: What's that supposed to mean?

PONY: I say what I mean.

SOOZE: You think you're so smart.

PONY: That's because I am.

(Sooze walks around behind the store, facing into the darkness, "the woods")

SOOZE: See how it gets dark down there, through those little trees and shit. What do you think is down there?

PONY: Old tires? Bottles?

SOOZE: When I was a little girl, all those condos over there were woods. And a big stream ran down there. And a small pond.

PONY: Where's the stream now?

SOOZE: Who knows? It's probably drained into a pipe underground, we just can't see it.

(Pony grabs some food, hauls himself up onto the dumpster and listens to Sooze)

I had a brother who was, you know, retarded? Down's syndrome. We called him "Mikey," like from that commer-

cial, "Mikey will eat it. Mikey will eat anything." Mikey
was always eating because he wasn't that good at doing
things. He could walk places by himself, that was it. It was
safe to let him do that in those days.

So he used to walk down here in the afternoon and this
lady who worked in the bakery would give him a doughnut and he would sit on the steps and eat the doughnut. I
think the lady used to talk to him. And he liked that.
Mikey was getting pretty fat from all the doughnuts and
shit, but you figure, let him have his fun, you know?

That winter it got wicked cold and that same year the
bakery closed. No more nice lady. No more doughnuts.
But Mikey'd still come down here, looking for the doughnut lady. And one day, Mikey didn't come home when he
was supposed to.

We didn't find him until the Spring when the ice melt-
ed. They figured he had fallen through the ice on the
pond. Then he got sucked under, down the stream. He had
been pushed under the ice all the way down the stream to
a place where there was an old shopping cart some kids
had tossed in.

And there he was underwater in the rusty old cart, still
wearing his overalls, all decayed. But it was him.

(Pony has stopped eating, riveted by Sooze's story)

PONY: You found him?

SOOZE: No. Some kids. But I saw him.

PONY: Your own brother.

SOOZE: It was ten years ago. I'm over it. My mother's not, she
blames herself. All she does is watch the home shopping

network and drink. I keep telling her to go to therapy, you know? My Dad, I never see my Dad. Vietnam vet. I think he killed people over there. I used to wonder if Mikey was like his bad karma come back to get us. Anyway, he lives in Florida, skippers deep-sea fishing parties. *(Pause)* I hate it here. It's ugly. It's like being dead. You went away. I want to go away.

(Sooze is close to tears)

PONY: Yeah, "away." It's not always so great either. I mean, I don't want to come back, but I get homesick, sometimes.

SOOZE: Yeah? That's hard to imagine.

PONY: No, it can be really hard. Tonight I had to do this interview and the things they ask are so stupid. But I do it, because the work's important, you know? I do it for the work. I have to protect the work.

SOOZE: But it's gotta be fun.

PONY: Sure. And it's hard. Every night a new city. Pressure from my manager and my lawyer to write new stuff. I'll write a beautiful song and they're like: "But what will the video look like?"

SOOZE: Or the album cover.

PONY: Or the album cover. *(Smiles at her)* Sometimes I try to remember why I left in the first place. I think about people. I wonder what they're doing. I thought about you. Alot.

SOOZE: Me?

PONY: I did.

SOOZE: Yeah, when you called, I thought, there's a name from the past.

PONY: Or a name from the future.

(Pause. Tension)

I mean, we'll be working on the cover, right?

(Voices off)

SOOZE: I know what you're saying.
PONY: You do?
SOOZE: I like you too, Pony.

(Sooze walks up to Pony, takes his hand. She looks him in the eyes. Her tears have become a stone-cold intensity)

My mother has a saying: "Don't write any checks you can't cash."
PONY: Sooze . . .

(Jeff enters)

JEFF: He won't let me take him home.

(Buff enters, carrying a plaster "lawn gnome")

BUFF: On behalf of Burnfield I present you with the keys to the city!

(Tim climbs down off the roof and calmly walks over to the food and starts picking through it. He has reached a state of drunkenness where he looks almost completely straight)

TIM: What's to eat? I'm starving.

(Tim picks up a carton and picks at it. Buff grabs a beer and pops it)

BUFF: Gotta settle my stomach.
TIM: How was the limo ride? Thrilling?
SOOZE: It was the nicest thing I've done in a long time.
TIM: Good. Very good.
PONY: Where's Erica?

(Tim picks out a rib, sits on his spot and eats it)

TIM: Erica? She said she was feeling tired. Went back to the hotel.
PONY: Oh. *(Puzzled)* How did she get back?
TIM: I called Bucky's and got her a cab.
PONY: Oh.
TIM: Did you get hot mustard?
PONY: I gotta go out to the car for a sec. I'll be right back.

(Pony exits toward the limo. Buff shouts into Tim's ear)

BUFF: JUMP AROUND! JUMP AROUND!

(Tim takes a swipe at Buff)

TIM: Fuck off!

(Jeff approaches Sooze)

JEFF: I have to talk to you. There's something I figured out.

SOOZE: You smell like whiskey.

JEFF: No. Listen. We have to talk.

SOOZE: Is that a threat?

TIM: I ate a dog in Thailand. It tasted alot like this sparerib.

JEFF: I thought about New York.

SOOZE: Forget New York. I don't want to talk about New York anymore.

TIM: There was a restaurant where they served live monkey brains. The monkey is tied down and people eat its brains while it's still alive. I tried to get in, but I didn't have any money with me. And my mother has a saying: "Don't write any checks you can't cash."

JEFF: Tim, what are you talking about?

TIM: Ask your girlfriend.

(Pony reenters)

PONY: I called Erica's beeper. No answer.

TIM: What are you, her dad? She said she might go for a drink first.

PONY: She always answers her beeper.

TIM: She's a big girl. She's alright.

PONY: What did she say?

TIM: About what?

PONY: About where she went. What bar?

TIM: I don't know. The bar at the hotel.

PONY: The bar at the hotel. She told you this? What exactly did she tell you?

TIM: Well, dad, she told me she wanted to suck my cock.

PONY: Oh. Uh-huh.

TIM: She told me you wanted to suck my cock, too.

(Pony and Sooze exchange glances)

PONY: I think I gotta go.

TIM: Don't go! Aren't you going to suck my cock?

PONY *(Ignoring Tim, speaking to Sooze)*: I'm gonna go back to the hotel and make sure she's alright.

TIM: She's fine. Don't you believe me?

PONY: I think you're a sick fuck.

TIM: Blow me.

PONY: Fuck you, I never did anything to you.

(Tim throws his rib to the ground and leaps to his feet)

TIM: Watch your language, chief, or I might have to.

(Pony turns to go, picks up his guitar. Tim rushes after Pony, drunkenly puts his arm around him)

Wait, wait, wait! I'm sorry. I was just screwing with you, man! You rock stars are so sensitive!

SOOZE *(To Pony)*: Could you give me ride?

TIM: That's it! Give her a ride! That would be nice! You could give her a nice ride in the back seat all the way back to the hotel.

BUFF: In the limo!

SOOZE: Tim, go throw up somewhere.

PONY: You know what? It's none of your business what I do.

TIM: None of my business? You're fucking my best friend's girlfriend and it's none of my business?

SOOZE: What the fuck are you talking about?

PONY: Nobody's fucking anybody.

TIM: You're fucking with me. You're fucking with my best
friend.

(Tim gets in Pony's face, balls his fist)

PONY: You hit me, my lawyer will drop an assault charge on
you faster than you can say A.A.

TIM: Your lawyer?

PONY: My lawyer.

(Pony walks away from Tim as Jeff moves in on Sooze)

JEFF: Wait a minute. What are you doing, Sooze?

SOOZE: I'm leaving with Pony. Is that alright with you? Do I
have your permission? Or maybe you have to "think"
about it.

JEFF: Where are you going?

SOOZE: For a ride!

JEFF: Away?

SOOZE: Yeah, *away*. Away. Away. Away!!!

JEFF: To his hotel?

SOOZE: Shit, Jeff!

JEFF: So you can do an album cover?

SOOZE: Jeff, I've run out of words.

JEFF: Are you telling me something?

SOOZE: I don't know. And I don't care that I don't know.

JEFF: So, what about us?

SOOZE: What about us? I'm moving away, you're staying here.

JEFF: Maybe.

SOOZE: Oh, so now it's "maybe." You think I'm with somebody
else so now it's "maybe."

JEFF: No!

SOOZE *(Marveling)*: Wow. Wow. You're unbelievable.

JEFF: I was thinking . . . I figured something out.

SOOZE: I bet you did.

JEFF: Hey, you know what? Do what you want! Go with him.

(Pony puts on his diplomatic smile)

PONY: Hey, man. We're just going for a ride.

BUFF: In the limo!

JEFF: Oh yeah?

PONY: Yeah. That's all.

TIM: What's your lawyer's number? Gimme his number, I'll call him right now!

(Pony meets Sooze's eyes. Grabs her hand)

PONY: Come on, Sooze. Let's go.

SOOZE: Bye Jeff.

(Jeff has turned away. Disgusted)

JEFF: Just go.

SOOZE: What?

JEFF: Just go.

(Sooze goes right up into Jeff's face, almost in tears)

SOOZE: You really suck, you know that?

JEFF: Go.

(Pony and Sooze leave. Jeff's knees buckle under him and he ends up sitting next to Tim on the curb, surrounded by the trash that Jeff spilled earlier, now compounded by the Chinese food cartons.

In the course of this scene, Bee-Bee has become virtually a part of the woodwork, hidden in shadows. We've forgotten her sitting there.

Tim brings out the purloined bottle of Jack Daniels)

TIM: A toast to womanhood.

(Tim drinks and passes the bottle to Jeff. Jeff takes a long hit)

Without suffering, Jeff, you will never have knowledge.

JEFF: I'm not suffering, because I'm not jealous of Pony.

TIM: That's because you're a coward.

JEFF: No. I don't want her, not who she is now.

(Tim goes into overdrive, finally throwing Chinese food at him as he hounds Jeff)

TIM: You're a coward. It's lying there right in front of you, but you have to think about it.

JEFF: No.

TIM: You're a paralyzed baby. You wouldn't last two minutes in a prison, in a concentration camp. The ones who survive don't think, they just act.

JEFF: It's good to think.

TIM: You say "think," you mean "fear." It's like a black rubber bag over your head. That's all it is. All your philosophy's just there to cover the obvious.

JEFF: No. I understand something now. It's no big deal.

TIM: No, it's no big deal. The guy probably has his arm around her right now. Holding her close, nudging her tit with his finger. He's probably talking about "the revolution" and she's looking up at him with her big eyes.

(Jeff ponders the image. Stunned, he stands)

JEFF: No.

TIM: In a few minutes they'll be in his suite. They'll talk for a while. Maybe they'll talk for hours. About life, about their "work." They'll feel close and warm with each other. She'll start to trust him. They'll decide to sleep with each other but "not do anything." By six AM, I bet they're making the beast with two backs.

(Jeff is lost. He wanders, sees the Chinese food on himself)

JEFF: Fuck!

TIM: It's human nature, Jeff. She can't help herself and he can't help himself.

JEFF: But Tim, what should I do?

TIM: I'll lend you my .45. Blow his brains out.

JEFF *(Nauseous)*: Seriously.

TIM: I'm serious. Kill him or kill her.

JEFF: Kill me.

TIM: You don't have the guts.

JEFF: I don't feel so good.

(Tim grabs him by the face and pulls him to him, making him listen)

TIM: Because you don't want to admit what you *are*. Drink the last beer, go home, have a piss, jerk off and pass out. And you will have completed your mission on earth for one more day. It's the way it is, pal, it's the way it is. *(Starts to leave)*

JEFF: Tim?

(Tim stops)

What happened to you and Erica?

TIM: Nothing.

JEFF: Nothing? Really?

(Pause)

TIM: I'll tell you if you keep it to yourself.

JEFF: What happened?

TIM: I had her around back in the van, and it's going hot and heavy. She's this animal.

JEFF: Yeah?

(Tim looks at Jeff waiting expectantly for the rest of the story)

TIM: And I looked down at her and suddenly I was filled with disgust.

JEFF: Disgust?

(Tim gets up, pacing)

TIM: I got up, and she started hanging on me. She's crying: "Tim, Tim! Come back, I love you. What's wrong?" She wouldn't let go. And I looked down at her stupid face. Her stupid eyes. Her stupid mouth.

(Pause)

JEFF: Yeah?
TIM: And I hit her. *(Pause)* She wouldn't let go.
JEFF: You hit her.

(Tim is facing away from Jeff)

TIM: I guess. I was drunk.
JEFF: You don't know? How many times did you hit her?

(Tim turns and looks at Jeff)

TIM: She wasn't moving. I hit her until she wasn't moving. She's still back there. *(Pause)* Go take a look.

(Jeff is frozen, looking at Tim)

JEFF: She's unconscious?
TIM: I'm going home. I have a hard day of drinking tomorrow.
JEFF: Wait, Tim, what are you saying? Why isn't she moving?
TIM: Take a look. See for yourself if you don't believe me.

JEFF: Tim? You didn't . . . ?

TIM: Go look. Do you have the guts to take a look?

(Tim leaves. Jeff starts to move toward the back, then stops. He's stuck. He views the mess lying all around him and halfheartedly starts to pick up the Chinese food containers and throws them in the garbage can. But suddenly he stops and walks back behind the store, toward the van.

Bee-Bee moves out of the shadows, picks up the Jack Daniels bottle and swigs it.

Blackout)

ACT
FOUR

Morning. The store is open for business.

Norman is picking up the trash and wreckage strewn about. Pakeesa works the counter. Norman doesn't notice Jeff, sitting around the corner behind the store.

Buff enters, bounces past Norman up to the pay phone and checks the coin return for quarters. Amazingly, he finds some change.

Buff enters the store, buys a package of "Devil Dogs," comes out of the store and stands eating the gunk as he watches Norman working. Buff's attention drifts off.

BUFF: Beautiful fucking day, man.

(Buff finishes the Devil Dogs, drops the crumpled package where he stands, scratches his stomach and stretches. Then, before Norman can react, Buff scoops up his trash)

Sorry, chief. *(Takes a standing jump shot at trash can from fifteen feet. The garbage sails into the can)* Swish! *(Turns to go)*

NORMAN: That's OK for you. That's OK. Enjoy yourself.

(Buff turns, surprised to hear Norman speaking)

BUFF: You talking to me?

NORMAN: That's OK.

BUFF: Good, I'm glad it's OK.

NORMAN: When I get my engineering degree and I'm swimming in my swimming pool it will be very fucking OK.

BUFF: Hey, if you're talking to me, make some sense. I don't speak Swahili.

(Norman is picking up trash and throwing it into the dumpster)

NORMAN: In two more years, I will have an engineering degree. We will sell the store and we will move away from Burnfield, and the store and you standing here.

BUFF: Good. See you later. *(Turns to go again)*

NORMAN: You are a drunk and a bum.

(Buff turns)

BUFF: Your sister sucks my cock every night, swallows my cum and loves it.

(Norman doesn't get angry. Instead, he focuses his eyes as if trying to read fine print on Buff's forehead)

NORMAN: That's OK. We have a saying back where I come from: "Either the salt is rotten or the meat."

(Pause as Buff tries to figure that one out)

BUFF: You're not so smart, chief. I'm moving out to L.A.

NORMAN: That's nice. They have many 7-Elevens there for you to stand in front of.

(Norman goes back inside the store. Buff looks up and sees Jeff lurking by the pay phone)

BUFF: Hey man.

JEFF: Hey.

BUFF: Whoa, you look like shit. Didn't you go home last night?

JEFF: No.

BUFF: Your dad's gonna wonder what happened to the car.

(Jeff says nothing, only turns to look at Buff, amazed by the absurdity of his observation)

You know what we need? A hot cup of coffee. Hang on. I was up all night too, man. Long, long night.

(Buff bops up and into the store. As he mixes up a couple of cups of coffee with milk and sugar, Jeff approaches the pay phone, dials)

JEFF: Yes, uh, I'd like to report . . . excuse me? Yeah. Hello? Yes, I'd like to report a . . . a . . . crime. Why do I have to tell you my name? No, it's not in progress, it happened already. Well, no I didn't see it exactly. No. I had nothing do with it! Yeah, OK, I'll wait.

(Buff returns after flirting with Pakeesa)

BUFF: Calling Sooze?

JEFF: No.

BUFF: She stayed at the Four Seasons last night. But you shouldn't worry about that.

JEFF: I'm not.

BUFF: Life is too short, you know?

JEFF: I'm *not*. Worrying.

BUFF: Good.

(Jeff, tired of waiting, hangs up the phone. He comes over and sits next to Buff at the bench as Buff hands him his coffee)

JEFF: Buff, if I tell you something, would you promise not to tell anyone?

BUFF: Sure.

JEFF: I mean no one.

BUFF: Hey, you know me.

JEFF: This is serious.

BUFF: Yeah?

JEFF: Last night . . .

BUFF: I should have stuck up for you man, I know. You're my friend, she's your old lady. I feel bad about that. But I was busy, you know?

JEFF: No, this isn't about Sooze . . . she stayed at the hotel with Pony, huh?

BUFF: We *all* stayed at the hotel, man. It was party-time. I hung out with Danny, Pony's manager? Really nice guy. We talked about the video. They want a raw look, you know? Something fresh. Danny said if I can capture the reality of Burnfield, it would make a great tape.

JEFF: Buff, listen to me for a second . . .

BUFF: I know what you're going to say. I don't know anything about making a video. But that's a plus because since I'm just starting out, I have a fresh point of view. Which is good, you know, for marketing and demographics . . .

JEFF: Buff . . .

BUFF: But, hey, I'd do it for free, you know, just for my reel.

JEFF: Yeah, OK. But listen to me—

BUFF: —and guess who showed up?

JEFF: No. *Wait a second!* I have to tell you this. Tim . . .

BUFF *(Concentrating)*: Yeah, Tim.

JEFF: No, Tim . . . Tim is in trouble . . .

BUFF: I know, man.

JEFF: You know?

BUFF: That's what I'm trying to tell you. That chick Erica . . .

JEFF: They're looking for her?

BUFF: No, man! She showed up at the hotel! And we had this great time together. I stayed in her room last night. What can I say?

JEFF: You saw Erica last night?

BUFF: I saw *all* of Erica last night.

JEFF: Buff, stop making shit up. It didn't happen.

BUFF: Sure it did.

JEFF: Erica's in the back, in the van. *(Pulls Erica's cellular phone from his pocket)* Yeah, I mean, look, I found this on the path back there. It's her cell phone. She's in the van. I didn't have the guts to look. She's dead.

BUFF *(Panicked)*: She's dead!?

JEFF: Tim confessed to me last night. He was with her last night.

(Buff jumps up, agitated, walks toward the curb)

BUFF: Tim?

JEFF: Killed her.

BUFF: Bullshit!

JEFF: It's true.

BUFF: Total and utter bullshit. Look!

(Erica enters. Fresh, up, smiling, happy)

ERICA: Good morning!

(Erica and Buff kiss. She pulls him close and grabs his ass. They remain in a loose embrace eyeing each other)

Don't look at me, I'm a mess. I'm completely burnt out!

BUFF: How'd you get burnt out?

ERICA *(Smiling, coy)*: Playing with something *very* hot.

(Erica notices Jeff. She sees her cell phone)

Oh, my God, you found it! Thank you so much!

(She takes the phone out of Jeff's limp fingers)

Jeff, have you been here all night?

JEFF: More or less.

(Erica immerses herself in Buff once more)

ERICA: Amazing. *(To Buff)* Did you get your tape?

BUFF: Yup.

ERICA: Don't you have a bag or anything?

BUFF: I have my toothbrush.

ERICA: He's so cute!

(Erica smiles a deep smile at Buff, very turned on by his completely loose ways)

BUFF *(To Jeff)*: I have to show my video to Danny at the hotel. If I get the gig, Erica's gonna teach me how to surf. In L.A.

ERICA: I'll teach you to surf, even if you don't get the gig.

(Buff is beaming)

BUFF: I can come visit?

ERICA: You better.

(They fall into each other's eyes. They kiss. Erica gets self-conscious in front of Jeff)

I'll wait for you in the limo.

BUFF: OK.

ERICA: It was nice meeting you, Jeff. If you're ever in Los Angeles you should come by the offices. I talked to Pony this morning and he told me he had a nice time last night and he's really looking forward to reading your songs.

JEFF: Tell Pony to fuck himself.

ERICA *(Sunny)*: I'll do that.

(Erica turns smartly, gives Buff a "hurry-up" look and exits. Buff watches her go, waits a beat and turns to Jeff)

BUFF: *The li-mo!*

(Buff bops over and sits next to the defeated Jeff)

See, man, I wasn't making shit up.

JEFF: No.

BUFF *(Reading his thoughts)*: Tim lied to you man, he was begging her to stay. She was laughing her ass off about it, you know? He did this whole macho thing on her head and then got pissed-off because she wouldn't suck his limp alcoholic dick. She told me all about it, man. Said he was crying 'cause he couldn't get it up. The guy's sad.

(Buff spies Tim arriving with a six-pack)

Oh shit!

(Tim sits in his spot. The three are in a similar position to their postures in the beginning of the play. Nothing is said. Tim drinks. Buff breaks the silence. He stands)

So, dude, I'll see you. And listen, if I never come back, I'll send you a video of me surfin'. Get some rest man. Go with the flow. *(Splits)*

TIM: So, did I call it? She stayed the night, didn't she?

JEFF: You lied to me.

TIM: You know what's wrong with you, Jeff? You want to believe so bad you'll buy anything. You're gullible and you're gutless, which is . . .

JEFF: No. No, that isn't the way it is, at all. I stayed up all night trying to figure out how to protect my best friend. I was trying to come up with some lie so you wouldn't have to go to jail for the rest of your life.

TIM: You did that? For me?

JEFF: Yes.

TIM: Then all I can say, Jeff, is you're a fool.

JEFF: Why? Because I give a shit? Because I care about you?

TIM: Grow up. You didn't even have the guts to go back and look in the van. Did you?

(Jeff jumps up)

JEFF: No. No. *Fuck that!* You lied to me. You lied to me because you're gutless. You're a gutless, drunken loser.

(A line has been crossed. Tim looks up with weary eyes)

TIM: I'm a drunk. And I'm a loser. But I'm not gutless. *(Drinks)*

JEFF: It's ten o'clock in the morning. What are you drinking for?

TIM: She took me into that van. Little Jewish Princess took me into the van, and she laughed at me. I'm tired of being laughed at. The pilots, the people with money, these greaseballs. Let me ask you something, Jeff: you saw that brown bitch point her gun at me yesterday. You think she was going to use it?

JEFF: I don't know.

TIM: You think after we left, her and Mohammed had a nice laugh?

JEFF: No.

TIM: Well, I disagree. I think they did. I think he probably went out with their friends later and all had a good laugh about the drunk on the corner. Makes me sick.

(Tim reaches under his sweatshirt and pulls out a Colt .45, looks at it sadly)

JEFF: Go home. Stop drinking. Go home and sleep it off.

TIM: Sleep what off? What should I sleep off, Jeff? My life? I should go home and go to sleep and when I wake up, what will I be? A pilot? A Super Bowl quarterback? Maybe a rock star? I don't think so.

JEFF: Just go home.

TIM: This is my home.

JEFF: What good does it do to start this? They never hurt you.

(Tim leaps to his feet)

TIM: Sure they have. Every day! They hurt me every day, with their attitude. Who the fuck do they think they are? I was born here. I had a life! They took it from me.

JEFF: They're people. They have feelings.

TIM: What about my feelings? What about my FUCKING FEELINGS?

(Pakeesa has alerted Norman, and Norman is emerging from the store)

THEY COME OVER HERE AND THEY KNOW ALL THE ANSWERS! AND THEY KNOW SHIT! WELL, I'M THE NEW TEACHER!

(Norman stops short when he sees the gun)

NORMAN: What is this now?

TIM: You call the cops I'll come in there and blow your fucking brains out.

NORMAN: I don't have to call the cops. We don't need the cops.

TIM: Call your sister. Have her fight your fights for you.

NORMAN: I don't have to call my sister.

(Jeff gets up to move away from Tim)

TIM: Stay there, Jeff.

(Tim lifts his gun and aims it at Norman)

How about this?

(Norman reaches behind his back where he has Pakeesa's .38 special in his waistband)

NORMAN: How about this? *(Norman aims the gun at Tim. Full of rage)* Go ahead, big man.

TIM: You fucking nigger.

NORMAN: Why do you call me names? I never hurt you. I'm just working here.

TIM: That's the problem.

(Jeff steps between them, blocking line of fire)

JEFF: Tim, wait a minute. What *is* your name?

NORMAN: What do you care?

JEFF: Maybe if we knew names, you know, things wouldn't get like this. My name is Jeff.

(Norman and Tim shift their positions attempting to keep a bead on one another as Jeff gets between them)

NORMAN: Norman.

JEFF: Norman what?

NORMAN: My name is Nazeer Chaudhry. Norman is . . . just a name.

JEFF: Nazeer! What's that, Indian?

TIM: Jeff, shut the fuck up!

NORMAN: Pakistani. Karachi is in Pakistan.

JEFF: You know, I wanted to ask you last night, Nazeer. You like living in America?

NORMAN: It's not a choice of whether I like it or not. I'm here.

TIM: Why don't you ask him if you can work in his store?

JEFF: Tim . . .

TIM: You have no respect for yourself.

NORMAN: Get off my property now.

TIM: You gonna shoot me? *(Backs up towards the dumpster, hitches himself up onto it, stands on it)* Now what you gonna do?

NORMAN: Get down off my property.

TIM: Fuck you!

NORMAN: I *will* call the police.

TIM: Go ahead! They love you almost as much as I do.

(Tim is on the roof)

NORMAN *(To Jeff)*: Tell him to come down.

JEFF: Tim, let's go.

TIM: Give me one good reason.

JEFF: I'm asking you.

TIM: You're a coward. I don't go anywhere with cowards. *(Holding the gun, gesturing grandly)* Hey Ma, look at me! I'm on the top of the world, Ma!

NORMAN: Get off my roof! You bum! You drunk!

(Pakeesa has come out of the store. She barks a few words at Norman in Urdu)

PAKEESA: Ye kya hoora hain? Hai allah! [Translation: "What is going on here? Oh, God!"]

TIM *(Singing)*: Here she comes to save the day!

NORMAN: Get down, now.

(Tim turns his back to Norman. Norman has a bead on him)

TIM: Shoot me! Shoot me, you fucking . . . *(Seems to buckle, as if he were having a seizure)* Wait! Oh . . . shit! Jeff!

NORMAN: Come on, what you doing? Enough! My sister called the police. They are coming.

TIM: Jeff! Come up here!

JEFF: Tim, you alright?

NORMAN: Get off my roof! You are worse than the blacks.

(Tim has fallen onto his knees, and is momentarily out of sight. When he stands again he no longer has his gun; instead, he is holding someone in his arms: Bee-Bee)

TIM: Jeff?

JEFF: Is that Bee-Bee?

NORMAN: See what happens? They go drinking on my roof!

(Tim slings her over his shoulder and climbs down off the roof. Pakeesa harps at Norman, hysterical)

PAKEESA: Is kambachat mulk me kahan pasadea? Ye sab thomare rajay se hoora hain! Me rapas jara in houm! Bus bohort hogaiya! [Translation: "Why have you trapped me in this horrible country? This is all your fault! I am going back! Enough!"]

NORMAN: Is she drunk? Take her home.

(Tim brings Bee-Bee down and gently unfolds her body on the ground. Jeff crouches over the body)

TIM: She's pretty cold. *(Looking at Norman)* I hope you're happy.

NORMAN: This has nothing to do with me. This . . . this drinking.

TIM: It has *everything* to do with you.

NORMAN: No, she went up . . .

TIM: It's *your* roof, it's *your* problem.

JEFF: Bee-Bee?

(Tim picks up the pay phone)

PAKEESA: Ye log bilgul pagal hogain. *(Pointing to Bee-Bee)* Theiko, theiko! [Translation: "These people are completely insane! Look! Look!" as if to say, "I told you so!"]

TIM *(On the phone)*: Sally? This is Tim. Hi. Listen, there's an emergency down the corner. *(To Norman)* You're fucked now, dude. *(On the phone)* I think it's an overdose or something. Yeah, you know, down by the mini-mall. Send an ambulance.

JEFF: They coming?

(Tim gets into Norman's face)

TIM: You're going to be so sorry you ever showed your brown face in this town.

(Jeff has been crouched over Bee-Bee)

JEFF: She doesn't have any pulse, Tim.

TIM: Just stay here and watch him. I think Stan's over the liquor store, maybe he has his truck.

(Tim exits. Pakeesa barks at Norman again and he realizes he's still holding his gun)

PAKEESA: Piston muje theitho. [Translation: "Give me the gun."]

(Norman passes the gun to Pakeesa, his eyes riveted to Bee-Bee's inert body. Pakeesa goes into the store)

NORMAN: This has nothing to do with me. You know. She went up by herself. I tell them over and over, don't go on the roof. Don't go on the roof. How is she?

JEFF: She's dead.

(Jeff is still, his eyes locked on Bee-Bee. Norman paces, becoming hysterical, then trying to calm himself)

NORMAN: Oh God! Oh God! See what happens? On my roof! See what happens? Oh God! The police are coming. My sister called the police but it is too late. She's not dead. They will come and take care of her. I'm going inside. Oh God! *(Goes into the store, screams from within, bursting with frustration)* You people are so stupid! *(Emerges from the store)* What is wrong with you?! Can you tell me? What?! What?! You don't know! Throw it all away! You throw it all away! What do you think is going to happen, what do you think? Oh, God. Oh, God.

(Norman again goes into the store, leaving Jeff alone with Bee-Bee. Sirens can be heard approaching.

Jeff picks up Bee-Bee's limp hand and holds it, gently)